Managing the Show

Inside the Responsibilities of Major
League Baseball's
General Managers

By Al Lautenslager

Woodbridge Publishers
1280 Lexington Ave STE 2
New York, NY 10028

First Edition

ISBN (Paperback): 978-1-916849-92-1

ISBN (Hardback): 978-1-916849-93-8

WOODBRIDGE
PUBLISHERS

Other Titles by Al Lautenslager

- Guerrilla Marketing in 30 Days – Entrepreneur Media

- Guerrilla Marketing in 30 Days Workbook – Entrepreneur Media

- The Ultimate Guide to Direct Marketing – Entrepreneur Media

- Kick It Up A Notch Marketing – Cameo Publications

- RE: The Book – Morgan James Publishing

- Market Like You Mean It – Entrepreneur Media

- Da Vinci Visits Today – Self-Published/Amazon

- A Day In The Life Of A Tuscany Winemaker–Self-Published/Amazon

(Attained the No. 1 ranking on Amazon –
Travel upon release)

- Baseball Confidential – Austin Macauley
  Publishers

To My Wife
Julie Ann Lautenslager

Thank you, Julie Ann.

This expression and dedication is for you.

Enjoy this dedication.

I love you.

Dedications

I've recently dedicated another book to my father, Alfred J. Lautenslager Sr., for his influence on me in baseball and life. I dedicated a book to my now-passed father-in-law, Max Simpson, who stood out among many as an appreciator of writing, literature and thoughts in general. Both had significant influences on my life.

The dictionary defines dedication as the expression of friendly connection or thanks by the author towards another person. I add to this the word, influence.

With that dedication definition and my addition of influence, I dedicate this book to the one person more than or at least as important as the two people in my life mentioned above. That person is my lovely wife, Julie. To her, this book is dedicated. She is mentioned in the acknowledgements and is more important than just this book. To use a common expression, she is my rock, and I live with and for her to the fullest. She represents the words in the definition of dedication: friendly connection and influence.

Acknowledgments

With every book comes acknowledgements. I am all about love and thanks, and that's what these acknowledgements are for. The dictionary defines acknowledgements as accepting the truth or existence of something. I acknowledge and accept the truth that there are people who have helped me in my writing and publishing efforts. My wife, Julie Ann, is always first. She is first in everything in my life, so she is also first in these acknowledgements. Thank you for your love and support and, most importantly, for always standing with me in life. I love you.

Second, as always, the ABC: Allison, Bradley and Courtney come. You are all always in my thoughts as the best children to support their dad/stepdad.

Many baseball General Managers were interviewed for this book. They are all listed within. To them, I offer my greatest appreciation for your willingness to help, support and inspire me to write on this subject. Each one was forthcoming, honest, and passionate about what they shared with me. They are all the epitome of true professional baseball men, and it's a privilege and honor to know them.

Thanks also to all those who helped proofread, edit, print, and market this book. These individuals are too numerous to mention, but it does take a team. Thank you.

Lastly, to my animalistic support: Nola, in her shepherd ways, and Ivy, who still insists on being a cat. Treats all around. And as always, there is Lu.

Table of Contents

Introduction to Managing the Show   1

Chapter 1: Baseball — State of the Game   12

Chapter 2: Team organization and structure   19

Chapter 3: Assistant General Manager — Title and
       Responsibility   25

Chapter 4: MLB General Manager Duties   31

Chapter 5: Fred Claire — General Manager
       Extraordinaire   37

Chapter 6: Branch Rickey — Vision and Action   57

Chapter 7: Theo Epstein — The Definition of
       General Manager   65

Chapter 8: Player Contracts — Everything in
       Writing   73

Chapter 9: Salary Arbitration — One Necessary
       Evil   87

Chapter 10: Ned Colletti — A Lasting GM
       Fingerprint   94

Chapter 11: Nick Krall — Cincinnati Reds —
Follow the Path   103

Chapter 12: Bill Schmidt — Colorado Rockies —
Managing a Business Surrounded by
Passion   116

Chapter 13: Bob Howsam — Putting "Manager" in
General Manager   124

Chapter 14: Trades — Acquiring Players and
Building Rosters   130

Chapter 15: MLB Scouting — A GM Essential   145

Chapter 16: Player Development — General
Management of People   158

Chapter 17: General Management For the Trade
Deadline   171

Chapter 18: Analytics — Measuring the Sport   185

Chapter 19: Player — GM Relationships and
Interactions   194

Chapter 20: Dan Evans — A True Baseball
Authority   202

Chapter 21: Dick Williams Laid the Foundation for
Today's Successes   209

Chapter 22: Ben Cherington — From Player
            Development to Team Development214

Chapter 23: The Draft – Selecting the Future   222

Chapter 24: Free Agency – Part of the Roster
            Building Puzzle   233

Chapter 25: The Globalization of Baseball and
            International Players   242

Chapter 26: Winter and General Manager Meetings
            – Where Things Happen   249

Managing the Show - Conclusion   257

Introduction to Managing the Show

It's the dead of summer, my favorite season of all. I love the hot weather, patio dining, sitting outside, enjoying the sights, sounds and baseball. Every day, I wear one of my favorite team's baseball caps, jerseys, or shirts to go about my day.

Baseball makes me very happy. It puts me in a true state of bliss. Anything baseball, player stats, standings, watching games, team-level strategy, and on-the-field tactics, all of it brings me great delight every day. If a baseball game is not going on, I count the days until pitchers and catchers report to spring training.

If following or partaking in baseball doesn't make you happy, please do something that will instead. Nobody wants you to live your life being unhappy. If you are like me and baseball offers the potential to make you happy, then keep reading. Let me share my happiness with you. Let me share these parts of baseball with you. This is my gift to you.

Moneyball, another good baseball book by Michael Lewis, is filled with detailed insights into the ins and outs of baseball general management and a baseball franchise. These ins and outs are managed by a General Manager. In the case of Moneyball and the Oakland A's —the subject team of the book— the General Manager is Billy Beane.

Beane was considered the precursor of the trend that has swept the baseball world —sabermetrics. The Theo Epsteins, Jon Daniels, and Andrew Friedmans of the world might not be as well-known without Billy Beane. The idea behind the concept of what he was trying to do was to maximize performance without spending the big bucks by finding players that slip through the cracks, all in the spirit of the general management of the team.

He used these methods to find replacements for the money the team actually had. As his General Manager's duties entailed, Billy did everything that this book is about. He was a true General Manager. Forget his ways. The fundamentals were at play. Follow along here for those fundamentals, the experiences and more. Aside from all of this, Billy takes players who have made it to "The Show" and does something with them.

The Show, you say? Goes on.

Tune in to any MLB broadcast, radio, TV or streaming, and you will hear broadcasters and reporters, including "The Show," in their reporting.

John Sadak of the Reds says things like, "That's the first time for that player in the show."

He's also been heard to say many things about reds 2023 rookies doing exciting and first-time things in "The Show." Aside from Sadak, new rookie players are welcomed by all on their first day in the major leagues with the familiar greeting of "Welcome to the Show." Several social media sites will post banner welcome messages when a player reaches the big leagues, "Welcome to the Show!"

The Show in major league baseball terms is, in fact, the major leagues. This includes the American and National Leagues. Some say the big leagues. The Show is not the minor leagues where players play mostly in AAA, AA, and A-level leagues. Most play many seasons, if not years, in the minor leagues before their invitation to The Show. Regardless, every player remembers their debut, their first day being part of The Show. This is a frequent occurrence during the baseball season. The show is the pinnacle of a baseball career. Ask any minor leaguer what their goal is, and they will tell you: to get to The Show. They all want that promotion.

As I go through my summer baseball days, I am inundated (pleasantly so) with box scores, videos of game highlights, player interviews, media critiques, emails, and so much more from The Show. Right about the beginning of July, after the July 4th holiday, I had started hearing the start of the buzz about the MLB trade deadline, which in 2023 was August 1st. The buzz swelled from there. The material I read, watched, and experienced was flooded with anything and everything about the trade deadline, another opportunity for baseball's General Managers to develop their show further.

Every day, I would see many, many headlines like the following:

"Our team should be looking at another starter."

"If the Reds have any hope of playing in the postseason, they would be wise to get a veteran who has been in the middle of a post season and could help the rookies settle down and not break under pressure."

"Fans have been begging the Diamondbacks to make some moves before Tuesday's MLB trade deadline."

"We're officially in the waning hours of trade deadlines, and I haven't seen anything that even hints that we're prospecting to do anything to help us the remainder of the season!"

"This has got to be one of the most boring deadlines of recent memory."

The rhetoric goes on and on and on. It sure was feeding my desire for anything and everything baseball. The more I read, the more I put myself in the teams' General Managers' shoes. What would I do? Do I agree with the many sentiments? What moves will happen next?

In the Major League Baseball (MLB) world, the trade deadline is the time of year during the season that sends through the whole sport and all of its fandom, altering the course of teams and players alike. Trade deadline time is truly exhilarating, adrenaline-charged and a roller coaster of fan (players and teams) emotions. As the deadline approaches, down, sometimes to the last minute, teams frantically engage in negotiations, seeking the perfect deals to enhance their rosters and propel them towards that championship trophy. That period is a riveting scene that captures the attention of baseball fans, players, management, and enthusiasts worldwide, as it presents the opportunity for newsworthy trades, unexpected deals, and the emergence of potentially new challengers in the year's pennant race.

The trade deadline not only puts a spotlight on baseball buzz, but it puts a big-time focus on the General Manager of each team.

Just like armchair quarterbacks in football, we, as true baseball fans, put ourselves in the shoes of the team's General Manager, at least in our own minds or in the hot stove league conversations abound.

In football, an armchair quarterback is defined as someone who doesn't participate in an action but still makes judgements and offers advice or an opinion on something in which they have little or no expertise or involvement. Those types of participants exist in baseball, too. That's what we are during the trade deadline buzz period.

Just like back in the days, when Billy Beane brought the management of the Oakland A's to the forefront, and as in Moneyball, Twitter was awash with fans wondering just what A's General Manager Billy Beane was doing to their team. That same wonderment is ever-present today.

One of the side effects of the "Moneyball" era has been the glamorization (and, at times, charm and obsession) of baseball's General Manager position.

Agreed by many and as a cultural icon, Billy Beane may be the most famous General Manager in sports history. Not only did he beat the traditional baseball management system using statistical analysis, but he helped an entire industry understand and reexamine the way it was making decisions about how to put teams together, win games, and how to win it all.

Today, the same buzz is ever more present right before the trade deadline as fans and amateur (and professional, for that matter) prognosticators play MLB General Manager and guess, suggest, demand and pontificate what trades should be made, how a team should be made up and how to move to propel a team into playoff contention.

Consider this conversation (during the 2023 trade deadline season):

"In order to add pitchers like Verlander, Lorenzen, Snell and Hader, teams would have to make space on their 40-man roster. That's even before considering the 26-man roster (that's another general management challenge)."

"Players on the 60-day IL don't count against the 40-man limit. Some teams currently (at the time) have 47 players on the 40-man roster (7 of which are on the 60-day IL)."

"Optioning a player to Triple A does not remove them from the 40-man roster, even more strategic considerations."

"So, GMs consider who, currently on their 40-man roster, they are willing to give away in order to make room for any player the team acquires in a trade for prospects?"

"Adding a player or two today might involve tougher decisions than you'd think."

All these things are spinning in a General Manager's head times 100, 24/7.

We all like to play General Manager and talk about who we would trade to get favorite players and more, but there is more involved than a baseball-chess game.

General Managers do their business, sometimes behind the scenes. At other times, they are at the center of attention, either by fans, other teams, or the media.

Let's think about the cycle here:

The game is built on the premise that it entertains the fans. Fans watch in person, online or on TV. All teams and fans are striving for the playoffs that ultimately lead to the World Series Championship. Only one out of 30 teams make it to that ultimate goal. When the other teams do not, fans, media, players, and owners continue the cycle. Owners and fans alike question why their team did not win it all. Sometimes, it relates to individual player talent, team makeup, and how adjustments or reconstruction happened along the way. When fans look at all this, they start questioning, debating, and talking about how a General Manager did his job and how the team was constructed and reconstructed. That's why we are diving deep into the General Manager's job. Fans like to play General Manager and discuss what trades should be made and how fan favorites can be obtained to propel a team to the top, but few know what is underneath and behind. There is way more involved than bats, balls, and gloves.

George Constanza thought about that aforementioned chess game. He sat down with Jerry one day and started thinking out loud about what new job would suit him. George liked sports and other general hobbies. In his own way, George thought and expressed that he could be the next Billy Beane, GM of the Oakland A's.

The conversation with Jerry went like this:

Jerry: So, what are you gonna do now? You gonna look for something else in real estate?

Nobody's hiring now. The market's terrible. So, what are you gonna do?

George: I like sports. I could do something in sports. ⌈L⌉⌊SEP⌋

Jerry: Uh-huh. Uh-huh. In what capacity?

George: You know, like the General Manager of a baseball team or something.

Jerry: Yeah. Well, that…that could be tough to get. Well, it doesn't sound like you completely thought this through.

Yes, baseball general management is way more involved.

As I was inundated with massive amounts of information during the trade deadline period, I thought much about each baseball team's management strategy. Just like all other fans, I was playing General Manager every day. It made me think more about the game and really try to understand what the General Manager does, not only during the trade deadline period but in everyday baseball life. I decided to look more into that.

The *focus* of Managing the Show is the General Manager. Each team has one. Just like there are 30 different teams, there are 30 different types, styles, methods, sizes, and shapes of General Managers. Getting insight into each requires direct conversation with as many of them as possible, past and present. The rounding out of information comes from those interviews. Aside from that, there is much more information available for each that will be developed along with their direct input that will be told here.

We, as fans, think we know what to do, and we think we know what is going through the head of an MLB General Manager, but we really don't. We don't until now. **Managing the Show – Inside the Daily Responsibilities of Major League Baseball's General Managers** opens up the world of baseball general management and pulls back the curtain of what really happens in baseball and inside the world of a baseball General Manager.

Enjoy this book, and let's revisit it during the next trade opening day or the trade deadline season.

Chapter 1: Baseball — State of the Game

Hall of Famer, Rogers Hornsby, was asked once what he thought about as baseball's Opening Day approached.

His reply was succinct, to the point, and with great perspective.

Hornsby stated, "People ask me what I do in winter when there's no baseball. I'll tell you what I do. I stare out the window and wait for spring."

Spring has arrived, and so has major league baseball. That's the way I think and probably the way you think.

Major League Baseball's 2023 opening day opened with the Houston Astros unveiling their World Championship banner in Minute Maid Park. American League single-season record-holder Aaron Judge took the field as the Yankees battled the San Francisco Giants. For the first time since 1968, all 30 teams played their first games on the same day.

Max Scherzer stepped on the mound for the New York Mets against the Miami Marlins, reunited once again with fellow CY Young winner Justin

Verlander, although the 2023 August 1st trade deadline later in the year blew that pairing up.

MLB's new rules took center stage. The infield shift as we know it was gone. The bases in the game were bigger. A pitch timer was in place. What?

Baseball's Opening Day 2023 also brought the crack of the bat, the pop of the glove, the roar of the crowd, the smell of the grass, and many other baseball touches to our senses.

That's opening day; the only time all thirty teams will be undefeated before reality separates itself from fantasy.

That's baseball. That's baseball today. As we take it all in and experience the season in an ongoing nature, it's always good to ask: "What state is the game actually in?"

2023 brought on a slew of rule changes in play, as mentioned above, to speed up the pace of the game and encourage more action and scoring. There were other changes, but the pitch clock, larger bases, and a banned shift are the highlighted ones that contributed the most to the increased popularity of the game.

Because of the implementation of a pitch timer, games are shorter, solving one of the major ongoing complaints of baseball's popularity. Fans going to a game and fans in Eastern Time zones especially, hoping to see the end, can have a reasonable expectation for how long a complete game will take.

Fans have always asked for not only the quicker pace of the game, but they also wanted to see more action. This includes more stolen base attempts, more hits of all types, and corresponding defensive play. Things like the new rules related to pickoff limits, pitcher and batter disengagements, and defensive shift restrictions are attempts to influence more of that.

Aside from the pace of play and action, the state of baseball always has the debate between small-market teams and big-market teams on its agenda. That debate continues. Do you think a small payroll team can't get to the World Series? Consider the fact that the Tampa Bay Rays and Cleveland Guardians have each reached that World Series pinnacle in recent years. Many more examples can be seen daily and during the season.

In recent years, expansion has been a topic of conversation when discussing the state of the game.

In 2023, Commissioner Manfred stated that, "Expansion is coming, along with massive realignment, but first, baseball needs to find new ballparks for the A's and Rays, even if it means the A's relocating to Las Vegas."

He went on to say, "We need to be a more national product."

One solution heading into the new season is what he calls a balanced schedule. A balanced schedule in which every team plays each other. That's the current thinking and state without regard to MLB travel logistics and scheduling jobs and staff.

Some say America's favorite pastime is back, but it never went anywhere.

Many will argue whether that statement is true. At the time of this writing, MLB attendance was up nearly 9% in 2023 after rule changes. That is the highest since 1998. The 1998 spike was directly attributable to expansion to Arizona and Tampa Bay teams and the hotly contested home run race between Mark McGwire and Sammy Sosa. The 2023 rise is more widespread. Major League Baseball attendance is increasing at the highest rate in over two decades as fans continue to fill stadium stands this summer (2023).

On one Saturday in July, the league recorded its highest Saturday attendance in a decade. The league reported that over 1.5 million fans attended MLB games on another July weekend for a third consecutive weekend, leading to the first back-to-back weekends of at least 35,000 fans per game since 2015.

Another reason is that many teams are still in the playoff race. Add it all up, and Major League Baseball is trending in the right direction as far as capturing the American public's attention. That tells me Baseball is more than back and still claiming the title of America's pastime.

Rob Manfred: "Look, I think that the moniker of America's pastime belongs to our game," Manfred said, "and it doesn't really have to do with whether our ratings are the same as some other sport or not. Our game occupies a unique place in American culture."

Many of us agree with what Mark Van Sickle of Fan Nation – Inside the Kansas City Royals stated in 2021:

"Baseball is still America's pastime. Yes, the NFL and NBA may be more popular sports. Soccer is becoming increasingly popular every year in America. However, baseball is still the godfather of American sports."

Sure, TV ratings suggest otherwise. Van Sickle reported, "…but that metric ignores other strong indicators—like local fan-base fervor and enduring cultural relevance—that baseball still matters."

The state of baseball is good. Yes, there are challenges, but there have been challenges since the first day of baseball. Baseball is good and in flux. In fact, the state of baseball has never been more in flux.

The players on the field are more talented than ever before; pitchers pitch faster, batters hit harder and further. Much of this is driven by a new generation of exciting young stars emerging, which will fuel the interest of younger audiences and contribute to more relevance of the sport.

Major League Baseball is exploring new rules that could help solve issues such as pace-of-play issues and increasing offense by eliminating defensive shifts. Even large bases are now part of the fray. There is always the consideration of balancing ways to appeal to baseball traditionalists who are sometimes resistant to proposed changes.

The state of baseball always includes consideration of labor issues. It seems there is always talk of labor issues that could threaten to put a stop to games.

The game has challenges maintaining relevance in an increasingly fast-paced and competitive world. While the state of the game is good, it must, as it has over the years, continue to adapt. Let it be said with all these reports and this book that the state of baseball is very good, and you, me, and fans all over the world will continue to be entertained and fulfilled.

Chapter 2: Team organization and structure

Before we dive into the daily grind, the highs and lows, and the rewards of the job of General Manager, let's first take a quick look at the overall organizational structure of a Major League Baseball team.

Today, the sport is well into an era of free agency. With that comes sky-high salaries and compensation. Players, in these cases, are in the spotlight. The General Managers are out of the spotlight in most cases. They go about their jobs and stay focused and move on, straightforward, sometimes in the spotlight and sometimes behind the scenes.

The heart of any baseball team consists, first, of the players. They are the ones entertaining fans and the public. Players play for the name on the front of their jerseys and represent whatever brand or identity a team tries to promote. Aside from that, a set of executives and their staff put the roster of players together. Think of them as glorified "product managers."

All levels of baseball management require a specific skill set above and beyond creating a competitive team, above and beyond baseball operations, fiscal responsibility, and promoting the identity and the primary baseball product – the team and players.

This set of executives and team organizations vary in how many people are part of the front office team, their jobs, and what they are called (titles). Every single MLB organizational chart and staff description is different. Just go online and look up each team's staff. It is usually public and described.

Upon review of teams, some have a person at the top as the team's General Manager. In other cases, you will see the President of Baseball Operations or another similarly titled person who is the decision maker aside from the General Manager. It varies from team to team. Reviewing the team's structure will reveal positions such as Assistant General Manager, Director of Player Development, Scouting Director, Director of Analytics, Director of Baseball Operations, Special Assistant to the General Manager, and more.

Special assistant to the GM is a relatively new position that did not exist until after 2000. Now, almost every team in the league has several, often ex-players or ex-GMs, employed under this title. These positions generally report to the GM.

Typically and generally, a team will consist of a General Manager and two or three assistants second in command. After that, you will see scouting directors, player development, and baseball operations. There are also assistant directors or coordinators under each director. All have input and help with operations and decisions for team make-up. Again, this is average. For that matter, any General Manager or owner has discretion regarding the make-up of the overall organizational structure.

Needless to say, each team has a reasonably large and complex management structure. The best ones have clearly defined roles for each part and level of the organization. After this comes the whole make-up of the coaching staff, those responsible for managing the players and game each day of the season.

In January 2022, The Dodgers introduced Brandon Gomes as their new General Manager. Even then, in their announcement headline, there was ambiguity about the organizational structure and who was in charge of what. The headline read, in part, "…but how he'll (the new General Manager) divide duties with Andrew Friedman, President of baseball operations, remains to be seen."

Even with Gomes' promotion, the Dodgers' baseball operations organizational chart also includes many other titles/positions that confuse the average fan. On the organizational chart is a Senior Vice President, three people with the title of Vice President/Assistant GM, five additional Vice Presidents, 11 directors, three Assistant Directors, and five special assistants.

In most organizations, the General Manager has the final say regarding roster decisions. These include trades, signings of free agents, and drafts. In organizations that have a President of baseball operations, the General Manager is usually second in command.

In some cases, being a General Manager in Major League Baseball is not what it once was. The Red Sox are one of several organizations that have expanded their front office and hired a baseball executive who ranks higher than the GM. Looking at their organizational structure, you will see a Senior Vice President of baseball operations. Over the years, several teams have adopted this model or something similar.

Several General Managers operate with the titles of "President of baseball operations" and General Manager. Others have the title of General Manager but still report to Presidents of baseball operations who have final authority on team personnel, roster, and other team decisions. This varies from club to club, as not all of them have a baseball operations President.

According to Baseball America in its 2019 Baseball America Annual Directory, they listed 12 Presidents of baseball operations among the 30 MLB teams, as well as one "Chief Baseball Officer" and four "Executive Vice Presidents of baseball operations" operating above the General Manager level with just that title or also holding the GM title.

Steve Cohen, Owner of the New York Mets, stated that he feels the difference between the President of baseball operations and their General Manager "is the titles." In his organization, he envisioned a complementary relationship between their General Manager and a President of baseball operations, building on what Cohen considers a strong infrastructure in his organization.

In 2015, the Reds' President of baseball operations, Walt Jocketty, observed an interesting phenomenon in the meeting room at the Major League Baseball's General Managers Meeting. At the main table in one of their meetings, the Presidents of baseball operations were all in the senior section.

The General Managers were in the inner section. Some of those General Managers were the top decision-makers in their organizations; others were not. Titles did not necessarily correspond to job responsibilities. Teams still separate the two, and responsibilities vary. Also varying is the person who acts as the face of the organization.

When you see press conferences of player signings, especially the big names and big free agents, you will see the General Manager conducting them. The General Manager acts as the face of the baseball club in interacting with the media, making public appearances, and representing the team.

With all of this and the focus of this book, the General Manager position is what is concentrated upon. After all, there are 30 General Managers *in* Major League Baseball, as there are 30 Major League Baseball teams (15 are in each league).

For purposes of this book, the General Manager is in charge of "The Show."

Chapter 3: Assistant General Manager — Title and Responsibility

Look at any organizational chart and staff listing for any MLB team; you will see that it is more expansive than in previous years. That is the case for all 30 teams. Today, there are analysts, data management, logistics, and employees of all sorts to produce the baseball product.

One position title that has grown is the Assistant General Manager of the teams. While the focus of this book is the life of a General Manager, and while we discuss the organization and structure of teams, reviewing the Assistant General Manager position makes sense.

On average, in reviewing organizational charts, teams now have more than two assistant GMs.

In almost all cases, assistant GMs stay with their teams longer than any other management role.

Why, then, has the number of assistant GMs for teams grown?

There are many good baseball people making good baseball decisions and managing to build teams, but flat-out, they don't want to be in charge; they don't want to be General Manager. Their talent and work are still desired at a higher level, so slap an Assistant General Manager title on them.

Many work best in anonymity. Many want their job not to be subjected to the revolving door of many General Manager situations.

Other situations require what has become known as title inflation. Give those who have valued an Assistant General Manager title; the chances are better that they will be retained (or promoted) depending on club management. In view of that, you often see functional titles attached to the Assistant GM title. A good scouting director often comes with the assistant GM or VP title now, as do international scouting directors and other department heads.

Here are some examples of the Assistant General Manager title, responsibilities, and the coupling with other descriptions in the title:

In October of 2022, the Detroit Tigers hired Tampa Bay Rays' senior director of amateur scouting, Rob Metzler, as the organization's new Vice President and Assistant General Manager. It was announced that Metzler would lead the Tigers' amateur and international scouting efforts.

In February 2019, the Seattle Mariners promoted Joe Bohringer to Assistant General Manager. Bohringer's focus areas included overseeing the Mariners Analytics Departments and staff, the area of new Player Development Technologies, and the research and vetting of other new technologies in the baseball operations department. He was to be responsible for overseeing, delegating, providing quality control, and managing the budgets for all of these areas, as well as for Athlete Management and Research & Development. In addition, he was to serve as the primary liaison from the front office to all Medical Doctors, Specialists, and consultants. (Bohringer later left this Mariner's job after a year in the job).

In September 2023, The Chicago White Sox named former major league utility infielder Josh Barfield as assistant GM. (No other additional title or description of responsibilities)

In 2019, Ben Cherington, the Pittsburgh Pirates' General Manager, hired Steve Sanders as the Pittsburgh Pirates' new Assistant General Manager. Sanders came from a scouting and developing background and had a big role in Toronto's ability to successfully identify and draft promising young players. It was stated that he planned to spend time in those same areas for the Pirates.

Some assistant GMs have added Vice President to their title, like the Cincinnati Reds' Sam Grossman, who is Vice President Assistant General Manager for the Reds, and the San Francisco Giants' Senior Vice President & Assistant General Manager Jeremy Shelley.

The Washington Nationals have done this for three Assistant General Manager slots: Assistant General Manager & Vice President, Scouting Operations, Vice President & Assistant General Manager, Baseball Operations, and Assistant General Manager, Player Personnel.

The Baltimore Orioles have two Assistant General Managers on their organizational chart: Vice President and Assistant General Manager, Analytics, and Assistant General Manager, Baseball Operations.

The assistant GM captures a lot of different job descriptions and responsibilities. Assistant GMs typically are safe from competitive intruders and evolve into their best areas of work and concentration.

Some see the AGM role as a stepping stone to running a team and becoming a General Manager.

In the "old days," the Assistant General Manager spent most of his time helping manage the team's budget, coordinating team travel and baseball-related logistics, and arranging player housing, hotels, and transportation. The times have changed that.

In some staff directories, you will see assistant to the General Manager. This is different from being an Assistant General Manager. The Cincinnati Reds, for example, have various special assistants to various roles, including but not limited to advisors to the CEO, General Manager, player performance, and player development.

While things are ever-changing with the job, defining the Assistant General Manager's responsibilities, regardless of title, is key.

The Arizona Diamondbacks hired an Assistant General Manager in 2010 to provide a resource when working with players and their agents, especially as Arizona's young core of players reach arbitration age and go through that process. In this case, their assistant GM had very specific responsibilities associated with his title. He was expected to work closely with the scouting department in defining bonus recommendations surrounding the First-Year Player Draft each June.

When Chicago White Sox's new assistant GM was named, his key focus areas were player development, roster construction, and player acquisition. He is also expected to oversee the farm director role.

From reviewing all of this, it is clear to see that the Assistant General Manager position is varied and fills many clubs' organizational charts. The benefit, beyond functionality, is the promotability of each, as well as a notable standing and reputation within the industry.

To look at any staff organization listing, visit https://www.mlb.com/TEAM-NAME/team/front-office. Insert the name of the team whose listing you want to view in this link where it says "TEAM-NAME".

Chapter 4: MLB General Manager Duties

When looking at and living baseball in terms of player stats, standings, watching games, strategy at the team level, on-the-field tactics, and more, it all comes down to the management of all these things: the management of baseball. That's where the General Manager of each team comes in. A team's General Manager is responsible for many aspects of the team that eventually turns into a business that provides a baseball product and a true fan experience.

We will start very basic by looking at the responsibilities and duties of an MLB General Manager; then, we will look at some real-life situations and related stories.

At the heart of Managing the Show is the story of the job of the General Manager. This will take many forms, but essentially, it considers who makes the decisions in a baseball organization and, in the course of the job, who's second-guessed by fans, the media, and even players and who has to deal with unending and sometimes impossible expectations.

Being a General Manager is not an easy thing to do. A GM must put up with their boss's notions and quirks (the owner(s) of the team), they must acquire talent that will make their team better, and they have an ongoing job of monitoring and scouting the most players in any sport to acquire them, all while working towards a championship.

While all GMs must do these things and win to succeed, this sport stands out as it is the one that has a breed of General Managers who top all the rest.

Baseball players and coaches get the most credit for winning or losing. However, team rosters and coaches hired are all done and built by the GM, which sometimes gets lost when handing out credit. The GM (General Manager) works directly with the owner to spend their money as the owner would like.

Bob Howsam of the Cincinnati Reds in years past comes to mind. Howsam was the highly successful General Manager (GM) and Club President of the Cincinnati Reds during the Big Red Machine's winning years between 1967 and 1977, when the team won four National League pennants and two World Series titles.

While we talk about the duties and the expectations, Dan Evans states it best. Dan is the former Los Angeles Dodgers General Manager, among other baseball executive positions.

He states, "…a GM really does not know what to expect every day, and unlike most professions, must respond and lead without that certainty. Injuries, the postponing and canceling of games, potential trades and assignments, and unexpected ups and downs of a baseball season require a GM to be flexible while developing alternate plans for every situation. A GM prepares for these decisions by staying on top of everything that could affect the team, within and outside their organization, while relying on their staff to aid them in their decision-making.

You are leading a baseball organization from top to bottom, so philosophically and strategically, you can make an impact throughout your team, from player development to international scouting, your administrative staff, and professional and domestic scouting, along with how you continuously act and operate. It is especially tough from June through August when some organizations have as many as seven or eight minor league teams playing daily after the amateur draft."

We offer a discussion of what a GM does. It's a discussion instead of a total breakdown or list, as the duties, responsibilities, and structure vary from team to team.

We said it before, but it bears stating again the success of a baseball team comes down to the management of all the things listed under a GM's responsibilities: the management of baseball.

Team management allows them to move forward and keep fans interested. Again, this is providing a baseball product.

From outlining strategies for the direction of the team to hiring everyone on the team, they are in charge of, and surely, the captain of the ship.

A baseball team's General Manager, or GM, typically controls player transactions and is responsible for contract discussions with players. They are also the person who typically hires and fires the team manager and their coaching staff.

A GM handles day-to-day, hands-on duties with players and coaches while managing their team's short- and long-term future. This overall construction ranges from the minor leagues to the majors, such as The Big Show. For example, when the team manager needs a new pitcher or position player, the GM decides to send a player up from the Minor Leagues or seeks a player to trade for.

There are a few important, specific duties of a General Manager. Let's take a look at them:

- The GM spends the team's (owner's) money in a way the owner would like.

- Once the owner provides money to the General Manager, it's up to the General Manager to make decisions in the best interest of the ball club.

- It's up to the General Manager to buy and sell at the right time, acquiring the right talent. This may be before the MLB trade deadline is reached or in the off-season. They are responsible for negotiating player contracts that go along with trades and player acquisitions.

- General Managers not only invest in players, but they hire coaches for the team as well.

- They hire front office personnel like experts, assistants, scouts, analysts, and other front office personnel.

- A GM is responsible for monitoring and scouting other players in the sport, domestically or internationally, at all league and non-league levels. This includes free agents, first-year player draftees, and international prospects.

- Works with a team consisting of scouts, coaches, the assistant GM, the data analytics team, and other staff and front office personnel.

- Hiring those other front office personnel like analysts, scouts, PR, and financial people.

- A GM acts as the principal spokesperson for the organization.

- The General Manager oversees and negotiates contracts of team players.

The modern-day General Manager is inundated by texts and emails, voice mails, agent phone calls, media inquiries, and tweets while simultaneously keeping ownership up to date about budgets, player development, and the road to the World Series. He also monitors the progress of minor leaguers in the pipeline. Other than the week between Christmas and New Year's Day, breaks in the schedule are nonexistent. It truly is a 24/7 – 365 job, as many have mentioned along the way.

Add all this up, and the obligations and responsibilities of an MLB GM sometimes come with a challenge, and many times opportunistic and very wide-ranging.

Chapter 5: Fred Claire — General Manager Extraordinaire

Baseball players, coaches, managers, and general managers all have different paths that define their careers. We read about them in Managing the Show. Fred Claire's path falls into that other category and is worth reviewing and reading about.

The focus of Managing the Show is the General Manager. Each team has one. Just like there are 30 different teams, there are 30 different types, styles, methods, sizes, and shapes of General Managers. Getting insight into each requires direct conversation with as many of them as possible, past and present. The rounding out of knowledge and information comes from those interviews. Aside from that, there is much more information available for each that will be developed along with their direct input that will be told here.

Fred Claire has offered direct input as well as other sources of information related to his life as a General Manager.

Fred Claire spent 30 years with the Los Angeles Dodgers' front office, advancing from publicity director to Executive Vice President and General Manager.

Regardless of his position, Claire joined the Dodgers in 1969. Fred proved to be an award-winning executive at every stage of his career. Fred mentioned that he was directing the team's marketing efforts when the Dodgers first hit the three-million mark in attendance and established a period of record-setting attendance figures. He was proud to tell me he was instrumental in creating the branding that became to be known as "Dodger Blue."

Fred states that he has been blessed to see the evolution of the General Manager position from his days as a fan to being a part of the Dodgers organization and knowing many people, returning to the days of Branch Rickey.

Who, more than Fred, offers insight into the General Manager's position and Managing the Show in Major League Baseball? He did just that during my many recent conversations with him about that subject.

Before getting into the nitty gritty of baseball management from Fred, I think it's important to note one beginning mantra from Fred:

"The job of a General Manager is no different than any other job in one respect: It is the people we come home to who mean the most to us."

I also live by that. Thank you, Fred.

Now, onto the GM job.

Fred Claire describes a typical day much the same as most other General Managers. Managing all the moving parts and the complexities of a baseball team can seem unending and constantly in motion. Fred states that the job of the General Manager of a Major League Baseball team is a 24-7 job. I asked for a typical day, and he, like the others, point blank said, "There is no typical day." Each day and each time of the year/season brings on different challenges and opportunities.

The job entails the mindset, attitude, and work ethic set, as well as always doing anything in the very best way to improve the team. Along with this comes managing and working to improve the team's overall baseball operations. Sometimes, that is department-related, and sometimes, it overlaps with many places in the organization. Again, the time of the year and the point in a season brings about different challenges and tasks.

One point of fact related to the point of the seasons is that, as Fred states, there is no "off-season." Many have said there is spring training season, regular season, post-season, and the off-season. In the general management world, there is no off-season. When post-season play and activity come to an end, there is a critical period of final evaluation of players. It's not really final, as player evaluation is a continuing, ongoing activity. This happens during the season to construct a roster, replace players, and upgrade them. This is happening through free agency after the post-season or trades during the times allowed to trade.

General Managers start the all-out preparation for post-season play at the end of a season and even before the actual conclusion of play.

After post-season play comes regularly scheduled meetings of Major League executives. The General Manager meetings and the Winter meetings are key events. Representatives of all 30 Major League Baseball teams and their 120 Minor League Baseball affiliates convene for four days each December in the Winter Meetings to discuss league business and conduct off-season trades and transactions. The week of Winter Meetings is typically the busiest part of the off-season. These times are hectic but fun and productive, according to most.

After the Winter Meetings, Fred speaks about the Composure of the team for the upcoming season. Obviously, that composure is based on many things. At the forefront of that are meetings with the Major League staff, scouts in the organization at all levels, members of what most teams have, player development departments and teams and, in today's world, meetings with members of the analytical team.

Typically, during a day of the meetings, GMs and their staff spend time discussing business issues related to the game. There are conferences and meetings galore. Here, teams meet and talk about a team's priorities and to-do list, the going rate for players in the market, and things planned for the off-season, all while learning which team plans to do what and what players may be available.

In Fred's case and every other General Manager's case, they are there to find ways to improve their team, roster, and position in this offseason session. Fred reflects on his first time at the general management meetings as the man in charge of the Los Angeles Dodgers baseball operations. He knew what he wanted and had his shopping list at the ready. Typically, knowing trades could and would be made, Fred states that he wasn't afraid to make a move. He just wanted to make the right moves.

After the Winter Meetings and almost simultaneously, preparation for Spring Training is critical. Once the 40-man roster is in place, key decisions are made for non-roster players and spring training invitees who will be part of the team organization at spring training.

Fred has already said that a General Manager's job is never-ending. It truly is a 365-day-a-year gig.

Spring training is an opportunity to see how the team looks and how it could look as it's the group that a team is stuck with, at least for the next two months of a season or more. During spring training, there are plenty of questions related to the state of the roster to answer.

While every General Manager wants more and tweaks around spring training time, it is virtually a no-trade market time. However, General Managers are always on the lookout for second-level big league free agents and some minor league free agents that might be available. Sometimes, a General Manager is led to his daily transaction communication to see if what they need to be deeper with their roster suddenly appears on the waiver wire. Sometimes, "tweaks" like this can pay big dividends later in the season. Now you can see why Fred says that the preparation for spring training is a critical part of the year. The old adage here is that it's more about preparation than execution.

While this is not a day-to-day to-do list recipe review, the following is a look at other perspectives of various components of the General Manager's job offered by Fred Claire.

The Start of Fred's Baseball Passion:

Fred talks about his family a lot. His charge in life and work is based on his own high standard. Fred states that no matter how high sights in life are set, the distance to those sights and the roads traveled to those sights are largely determined by the foundation from which we left. In Fred's case and many others, that foundation is family and a young upbringing.

That includes friends who gathered with him often for the local neighborhood baseball game at the elementary school field nearby. That was the start of his baseball passion that burns continually like the hottest of fires, never to be put out. Most General Managers have a similar childhood story, a similar baseball start story and the same continuing fire and passion.

General Manager to General Manager Relationships:

It is not unusual for baseball General Managers to have a network and ties to other General Managers who end up being their potential trading partners.

Fred Claire mentioned that relationships with other teams' General Managers are critically important. Fred is of an older regime. He recalled for me a conversation he had with Kevin Towers, former General Manager of the San Diego Padres and the Arizona Diamondbacks.

Kevin told Fred, "You wouldn't believe how trades are made today."

Kevin was referring to trades he knew about that were made with another General Manager via text. Texting may or may not have a relationship underneath it. Fred kept repeating, "You need to build relationships." Many times, it's a situation of trading information. Knowing the mannerisms and traits of other General Managers is critical in exchanges and ongoing business. Some, like Fred, are direct and to the point. That type of trait does not mix well with a generalist or someone with more far-reaching thoughts and ideas.

Building relationships gets deals done, especially when opposing General Managers' thoughts have a common alignment.

Fred mentioned that not only did he and Sandy Alderson, GM of the A's at the time, share a love for baseball, but they were both avid runners. One morning job, they started talking baseball. They talked about what if's and possible returns on possible deals.

On an August day in 1987, as the Dodgers were fighting to stay out of last place, the team unloaded the then-struggling left-handed pitcher Rick Honeycutt to the Oakland A's for a player to be named later. That name was Tim Belcher, and he turned out to be a successful trade component. Fred Claire knew Sandy Alderson needed a left-handed pitcher. Even though it was Fred's first year as the Dodgers' General Manager, the trade happened because of jogging and the relationship between him and Alderson.

Music to a GM's ears - ownership's support of decisions:

General managers deal with many, many things coming from all directions. That's why you hear many of them say every day on the job is different; there is no recipe for the daily to-do list. Take Fred Claire's first game, where a player got injured, ended up on the disabled list and needed to be immediately replaced; time for the General Manager to step in. Because of his connections, he knew who might be available around the league and who could fit the bill of replacing the disabled player. Fred proposed a deal to do just that to owner Peter O'Malley on his second day on the job. Discussion ensued; suggestions were made for others to get involved and provide advice, but at the end of the day, Owner O'Malley said words to General Manager Claire that every general manager wants to hear.

O'Malley questioned the timing of the deal but stated, "I wouldn't do this at this time, but it's your call."

Subsequently, Fred's deal was agreed upon, and his new player was in the lineup that same evening. Replacement done. Fred did admit that he might have gotten carried away with his gusto and passion, but that was his jumping-off point for general management. His General Manager career was underway, and owner O'Malley allowed him to make the calls.

Trade made by new owner without the GM – Spirit and Credibility:

Fred talks about a trade that was made by a new owner of the team (Fox) without his involvement or knowledge. Fred was the General Manager. The process was changed or, better yet, ignored. Fox, the new owners, knew the business but did not know baseball trades. When Fox did that, it was big news in Dodgerland and all over baseball. It was deteriorating club morale. Fred stated that when a General Manager makes a bad trade (yes, that does happen), his spirit is damaged, especially with the level of dedication and passion of Fred Claire. When a trade is made without the knowledge of the General Manager (rare but happened with this new owner), his credibility, as Fred states, is shattered.

Is there an offseason for a General Manager?:

Once the season is over, all new thoughts go to the next season. In Fred's case, he was no longer committed to team play and wasn't traveling with them. Here is a sequence of his typical off-season activity and progression through the start of the season:

- Once the season ended, he went to instructional leagues and spent time with people there. Instructional leagues are effectively the future of the team.

- Visits to Winter baseball leagues and play. He made important trips, often, to Venezuela and the Dominican Republic. These trips were mainly to review those who might become free agents for the trade market.

- Preparation for the General Manager meetings. These happen right after the World Series.

- Following the General Manager meetings comes baseball's winter meetings. It is here that players are signed, deals are made, all for building the team's roster.

- By this time, it's January, and full attention goes into planning for Spring Training.

- Spring training brings involvement with the team and attendance at all the games.

- Between spring training and opening day, he spends a lot of time with his major and minor league staff and scouts.

- Then opening day happens.

Fred told the story that one year, late in the year, after signings were complete, he went to Hawaii for 7 days with his wife. This was right around Christmas time. That was his attempt at an offseason. Lo and behold, a deal was in the midst during that time. He completed a deal and called his publicity department to put out the announcement of the trade. They informed him that it was Christmas eve, and if he put out an announcement, all the writers and reporters would frown upon that, causing them to work on Christmas eve.

Fred's response was, "I don't care."

His policy was to announce a trade when it was made, regardless of the time.

All in all, and in view of his Hawaiian holiday, Fred Claire finally admitted that there really is no offseason. He was totally consumed with his work and loved every minute of it during his whole tenure as General Manager.

Another to-do item for General Managers:

Dodger owner O'Malley considered replacing Fred Claire after year one of his role as GM. Peter

O'Malley had his reasons, but Fred wanted to continue and didn't want to be replaced. After lots of discussions inside management circles and conversations that happened in these situations, O'Malley decided to stick with Fred Claire.

Fred stayed, looked ahead, and realized there was much "general management" type of work to be done. He knew his team's gaps and went to work to address them. The first place to do that was at a place where every General Manager attends, is active and looks forward to. That place is the General Manager's winter meetings. Always a place for active discussion, trades, and other conversations.

General Manager vs. President of Baseball Operations:

Titles are titles. There are many in an organization that have one title and end up doing many things outside of what that title would suggest. Titles related to the person in charge of a Major League baseball team have changed. Fred makes a strong statement that regardless of title, there should be one person who is responsible for the team roster. With this comes trades, contract negotiations, promotions, and cuts, all within a General Manager's job description.

Times in baseball change and are different each day:

Sometimes, General Managers have to deal with the Major League Baseball Players Association. Each year, their involvement or at least the involvement of their rules and policies comes more into play. It can be said then and said even today, times in baseball change and are different each day, especially when you throw in things like arbitrations and agent representation for players. General managers will say that, when it comes to agents, you can't live with them, and you can't live without them.

A season's recipe for success with credit due:

From a General Manager's perspective, Fred was asked one day and summed up a season of success. Here is his general management recipe:

- Talented players who rose to the occasion determined to succeed. Afterall, it is the General Manager's job to assemble, acquire and draft the right players for the right performance.

- Success was also due to the work of a scouting department and a player development department, both under the oversight of a team's

General Manager. Both departments, consistent with the General Manager's mission, work towards the same ultimate goal. That is not to be taken for granted.

• Success, of course, comes from a great job by the field manager, coaching staff, trainers, and other support.

• Last but not least, and maybe most importantly, a successful team and General Manager is backed by the financial and emotional support of the team owner, another component in the General Manager's recipe for success that is not to be taken for granted.

It's not all about the numbers:

Sometimes, a General Manager has to consider more than just numbers when evaluating and placing players on a team. Fred Claire had 43-year-old Don Sutton on the Dodger team. The numbers suggested that a 43-year-old past pitcher should not be on the team. The benefit in Fred's eyes of Sutton being on the team would be that Sutton would arrive to spring training and school every pitcher on the staff, especially the younger guys eager to learn about how to prepare for a season with a great work ethic. Don had learned this along the way with Dodger greats, and now he took on the role of giving back. Fred knew that. A General Manager knows things like that. Forty-three-year-old Don Sutton stayed on the team.

How to Deliver Bad News:

Fans want to know what is said to players when their time with the club comes to an end. Fred gets right to the point.

He told Darryl Strawberry one time, "Darryl, you won't be with the team. I want to meet with you tomorrow morning because we have come to the end of the road. You have failed to show the responsibility that is needed to be part of our team. You can bring any representatives you care to have with you."

That certainly is not a fun message to deliver to a player. That type of message is a clear message to any player.

Other General Manager Insight from Fred:

There is no cookie-cutter approach or path to what a General Manager's job is all about. Some of these examples show you that. There are even more things that baseball General Managers face during the season and in the offseason. Here are more of those:

• Dealing with players' emotions, especially players who had played their whole career for the team.

• The potential for work stoppage. There was a cancellation of the play in 1994. Teams were forced to use replacement players. In Fred's case, he told them their chance of making the major league team in non-strike years was only based on their ability. Fred states that as long as he is General Manager, to be clear, that's his policy. In subsequent times, when player issues arose and drama and politics raised their head, GM Fred Claire stepped in and clearly stated that until he was replaced, he would be making all player personnel decisions.

• Player injuries causing disruption in rosters.

- Example after example of a lot of team success and roster construction due to exceptional scouting.

- When dealing with a player requesting a trade, his comeback was genuine, honest, open, and very much to the point. Fred stated his first obligation was to the team, and he wouldn't trade or make deals unless it was for the benefit of the team, and he didn't mind repeating that when needed.

There is only one real goal in any season, and that's to win a world championship.

Baseball can break your heart if you let it.

The General Manager is in charge:

By now, you can tell that Fred Claire took his responsibilities to heart. When he became General Manager, he stipulated to owner Peter O'Malley that he, as General Manager, would have full and complete responsibility for baseball operations. O'Malley supported that wholeheartedly. Another thing never to take for granted in the world of general management.

The experiences and messages of Fred Claire are pronounced. That pronouncement is best summed up by a quote by Fred Claire in a previous interview:

"I feel very, very fortunate to have spent a lifetime in the game and meeting so many wonderful people. I called Vin Scully recently to wish him a happy 94th birthday. We had a wonderful conversation. Thinking of someone like Vinny, who devoted his life to the game. He started the way I did, as a fan. It's a game, but the real point of the game is the *people* of the game. That's why I tried to do everything I can to promote the game and give back the game. I want to encourage young people to get into the game. As a teacher, one of my main themes is to follow your passion. That's what I did with baseball." (Source: Rocco Constantino – ballnine.com).

Chapter 6: Branch Rickey — Vision and Action

A book on baseball general management wouldn't be complete without a mention of Branch Rickey.

You can look at a list of those who are or have been baseball General Managers, and a few immediately pop out, rise to the top and are most relevant and significant. Branch Rickey is one of those. Rickey was part of lots of baseball innovation and organizational infrastructure development.

There are many books, articles and essays written about Rickey. For this book, we will highlight those items that are pertinent and related to being a General Manager in managing the show.

As we look at baseball General Managers, we look for monumental trades, roster compilation, winning negotiations, and wins. Beyond the quantitative, there are conceptual shifts and events that General Managers once were a part of. Branch Rickey's general management of his teams consisted of his daily team management but also approaches and changes to the game over and above his own team's day-to-day   management.

This early baseball pioneer was instrumental in breaking Major League Baseball's color barrier by signing   Jackie   Robinson.   He   also created a framework for the modern minor league farm system and introduced the batting helmet. Rickey's career spanned many generations. He is noted for multiple revolutionary   changes   in   baseball. Branch Rickey was always looking to innovate.

His grandson, Branch B. Rickey, recalled.

"He was always lecturing, tutoring, motivating, cautioning,   and   inspiring."

Branch Rickey was one of the most important and charismatic figures in all of baseball, the classic prototype   for   all   General   Managers who would follow. His contributions to the game were both meaningful and highly significant.

In his heyday of general management in the 1920s and 1930s, Rickey perfected the farm system, now mostly known as the base of today's minor league system. In his development, a major league team controlled young, undeveloped players through its chain of minor league franchises.

It's been said, but it's worth stating again. Branch Rickey was a baseball genius. He was a General Manager for 42 consecutive years for the Browns, Cardinals, Dodgers, and Pirates. Rickey was known as a shrewd General Manager and coach, even though his own playing skills were limited. His team's wins and losses count for nothing against how much he did to shape the game. Rickey had an unparalleled understanding of the game, notable motivational techniques, and a standout philosophy of winning.

Rickey wasn't just a General Manager. He was once a player, team President, and part owner but is probably more known as one of baseball's chief innovators.

During his Pittsburgh tenure in 1953, the Pirates became the first team to permanently adopt batting helmets. That may not sound unusual by today's standards, but back then, Rickey proposed that players wear helmets on both offense and defense. Full disclosure: Rickey owned stock in the company producing the helmets. Within a few weeks, the team abandoned their use of helmets on defense; they were awkward and interfered with play, according to players. At that point, the trend of wearing helmets on defense disappeared totally from the game.

Aside from his general management duties, Rickey was best known for spearheading the integration of major league baseball in 1947, when he signed Jackie Robinson to play for the Brooklyn Dodgers.

Then, as the President and General Manager of the Brooklyn Dodgers, Rickey, knew that in order for baseball to be truly "the national pastime," the color barrier would have to be broken. A long tradition of white-only players would have to be broken.

Rickey's act broke the color barrier, going against an unwritten rule since the 1880s. It was reported that Rickey held tryouts for black players under the cover story of forming a new team in the USL called the "Brooklyn Brown Dodgers." Within this, his team was looking for the right man to break the color line.

In August of 1945, Rickey signed Robinson to a minor league contract. Preciously, Robinson was playing in the Negro leagues for the Kansas City Monarchs. In October of that same year, it was announced that Robinson would join the Montreal Royals, the Dodgers' International League affiliate, for the following 1946 season.

Jackie Robinson turned out to be a resounding success. He took all doubt from all naysayers. Robinson was baseball's first rookie of the year, and while he still wasn't the most popular with opposing baseball players, managers, and fans, he became extremely popular with the American public. His success became the crowning achievement of Branch Rickey's illustrious career. The newly formed, integrated Dodgers team would make the World Series that year. Although they lost in the World Series to the New York Yankees in seven games, Rickey's vision and action had set the stage for the Dodgers to be contenders for decades to come.

One of Rickey's innovative approaches as General Manager was revolutionizing spring training.

Rickey was not the first person to put his club through its paces in the spring before the regular season. "Cap" Anson gets the credit for that innovation (and we'll talk about him in another posting).

Even though Cap started spring training, Branch Rickey deserves and gets the credit for revolutionizing spring training.

Rickey, at the time, was with the Brooklyn Dodgers. In post-World War II times, he bought what was originally created as a Navy housing base and transformed it into the home of spring training for the Los Angeles Dodgers in Vero Beach, FL, which was known as Dodgertown (abandoned by the Dodgers in 2008).

It was in the front office and general management where Rickey found his calling. He invested in the purchases of several minor league teams and created a feeder system that is known today as the minor leagues or the "farm system." The farm system is what developed young players and seasoned them for the major leagues.

Rickey still was a General Manager. He performed many duties described in this book that General Managers do today. Rickey was a shrewd negotiation in his job. For the St. Louis Cardinals, he built contenders in the National League as a result of his negotiations. Good General Managers are good negotiators.

"It occurred to me that if I let myself get trapped in a room with Rickey, there was a strong possibility that he would still have the players I wanted, as well as my promissory note, and I would end up with two guys I had never heard of," said St. Louis Browns owner Bill Veeck.

Rickey's innovative spirit shined bright in Brooklyn. He encouraged the team to use batting cages, pitching machines, and batting helmets and foreshadowed the modern-day sabermetric movement by hiring a full-time statistical analyst.

One of my favorite baseball quotes came from Rickey. After presiding as General Manager over one last-place season with the Pirates, Rickey proposed cutting the pay of power-hitting superstar Ralph Kiner. Kiner, of course, objected. This set up Rickey's famous comeback: "Son, we could have finished last without you!"

Mark L. Armour of "In Pursuit of Pennants: Baseball Operations from Deadball to Moneyball," wrote, "As a General Manager, he dramatically changed how teams find and develop players, and what players are allowed to play the game. His place as the greatest GM in baseball history is secure."

While Branch Rickey passed on more than a half-century ago and played in the game more than a century ago, his lessons live on.

Branch Rickey was elected to the Hall of Fame in 1967.

Chapter 7: Theo Epstein — The Definition of General Manager

In doing the research for Managing the Show, many past (and current) General Managers came to the forefront. Many were accessible and graciously offered their story or information pertinent to the title. In some cases, not all desired targets were available for live interviews, yet they were still worth profiling. Theo Epstein is one of those.

There are volumes and volumes written about Theo, his life, experience, performance, and his successes. This will only be the veritable tip of the iceberg. It still is worth this mention.

When thinking of a baseball General Manager, two of them immediately come to mind, at least to the average avid baseball fan. Those two are Billy Beane and Theo Epstein. Billy Beane put baseball general management on the map because of the best-selling book, which was later made into the blockbuster movie Moneyball. Theo first comes to mind because he started out very young and notably went on to build two curse-breaking World Championship teams.

With that level of success, Epstein's general management methods and approaches are worth looking at.

Theo Epstein was named General Manager of the Boston Red Sox in 2002 as the youngest GM in baseball history (Jon Daniels of the Texas Rangers has since surpassed the mark). That fact alone showcased his ability to perform and excel in high-pressure situations.

Epstein is now known as the General Manager who famously built the team that ended the Red Sox's World Series drought, breaking the so-called "Curse of the Bambino" in 2004. That drought dates back to 1918.

Epstein was totally instrumental in that championship. In 2011, the Cubs hired Theo Epstein as their President of baseball operations. His job at the time, acting also as General Manager, was to build a championship team while changing the culture of the famous north side Chicago baseball team. Theo attained a changed culture and won a World Championship in 2016.

The changed team culture played a significant role in reaching Theo's team goals. That culture boiled down to creating a positive, cohesive environment which let players be themselves on their way to greatness.

Epstein stepped down from his role on the Chicago Cubs on November 20, 2020. Jed Hoyer, Epstein's long-time deputy, took over his position.

Fox Sports offered their viewpoints on the greatness of Theo Epstein's general management prowess and expertise.

The importance of scouting has been mentioned throughout Managing the Show. In this book, we call it a GM essential. Theo Epstein believed that, too. He was a good scout, was involved in player development, and dove right into baseball's new information age, sabermetrics, analytics, and statistically influenced management.

Epstein could immediately identify those players that could have great promise. From those, he put together winning rosters and teams. He could spot potential in players that others could not. That led him to the acquisitions he made.

Epstein loved the ideas behind Moneyball and patterned some of his work after General Manager Billy Beane. That was part of his scouting but not the only thing.

Theo had a way of scouting players by not only looking at statistics and on-the-field performance but also looking at the person. His greatest measurement of a person in his scouting work was to evaluate a player's response to adversity. Theo would say that if a player folded under pressure, he was off the scout list. If he responded positively, he rose in the charts of evaluation.

With scouting well in hand, Epstein shifted a bit and focused more on player development. He did that with the Chicago Cubs farm system.

More player development and general management were going on, but scouting was the start and one of the main basic points of his general management and success.

Another gem of success was major signings under Theo Epstein when in Boston.

Theo Epstein was swooped into the Boston whirlwind. First, he rid the organization of then-manager Grady Little. That was one of the first items on Epstein's to-do list before he could undertake his signings.

As things got underway in 2004, Epstein made another notable move. Whether popular or not, that move was an on-the-field personnel change, getting rid of shortstop Nomar Garciaparra. Theo had to make room for his next signing of Orlando Cabrera. Cabrera went on to first-year success for Boston. Count that as another notable Epstein signing.

In the spirit of more signings, Theo was responsible for the signing of David Ortiz, who transferred from the Minnesota Twins at the time. We all know of David's success in Boston and how he went on to become not only a Boston ambassador but also an ambassador to the whole sport of baseball.

So, counting those signings and another with first baseman Kevin Millar, they would become what has been described as key cogs for the team that went on to win the 2004 World Series Championship.

There were other notable additions, but these were the mainstays and one more checked box in Theo Epstein's general management plan and eventual championship.

Theo Epstein also made some pretty notable moves in the managerial (and coaching) department.

In Boston, Epstein released manager Grady Little. He then went on to hire Terry Francona. This was 2004. Did that move work out for Epstein?

Under Francona's management, Boston won two World Series titles (2004, 2007).

He also recognized issues with managers when he was in Chicago. Epstein let Mike Quade, Dale Sveum and Rick Renteria go all in an attempt to, as he states, "repair the clubhouse." He just knew that if he wanted to attain the goal of a championship, he had to start with managers. After this, he settled on Joe Maddon. The chemistry between Epstein and Maddon was top-notch. In the time Maddon was manager (2015), the Cubs made it to the postseason twice, winning the World Series once.

While it's nothing short of a coincidence that both Francona and Maddon were hired by Epstein, it goes without saying that both moves were prosperous and successful for his drought-ridden teams.

Epstein's next General Manager move is what he considered a roster reinvention.

Epstein's eye for talent is what sets him apart from other GMs. He showed that in both Boston, for the Red Sox, and Chicago, for the Cubs.

Epstein was one of the first in baseball to be a very strong advocate for using advanced analytics in baseball decision-making. His approach helped revolutionize data and analytical-driven strategies in his never-ending quest for a competitive edge.

He played a significant role in revolutionizing the use of data-driven strategies. The increasing use of data-driven strategies and innovative approaches was fast helping teams gain a competitive edge.

In 2012, after some mediocre to cold years, Epstein figured it was time to seriously reinvent the team. That alone is any General Manager's major decision. Figuring out team strategy and direction is at the top of a General Manager's to-do list.

While we won't go into each and every trade, cut and transfer to reinvent the team, it can be said that Epstein proceeded with his own vision in his own way. Some of the names in that mix were Anthony Rizzo, Pedro Strop, Jake Arrieta, Kris Bryant, Kyle Schwarber, Jon Lester, and Ben Zobrist. Any Cubs fan, or baseball fan, for that matter, will immediately recognize these names.

Because of all these moves and continual general management like that and the championships in Boston and Chicago, most baseball people are saying Epstein has already earned his place in Cooperstown.

Look up baseball General Manager in the dictionary, and don't be surprised if Theo Epstein's picture is not right beside the definition.

Chapter 8: Player Contracts — Everything in Writing

The world all around us today is filled with people, especially sports fans, who love to win and watch winners. Fans want and demand the best from their sports team. This includes player performance as well as managing the set-up of a team to win. The responsibility to provide winning teams for the fans falls on the owners and the general management of a team. Fans will cheer, support, and come to the ballparks when they see their hopes of winning fulfilled or have a feeling that their teams are going to do well.

Our brains are wired to respond to rewards. That is why it is important to celebrate winning. Look up winning, and you will see that it is related to the production of dopamine, a hormone in our brain linked to pleasure. Winning produces more dopamine. Sports and our winning teams are in play for all of us here.

The team's General Manager is the architect behind producing a winning team and the related strategic decision-making. The MLB GM is primarily responsible for player acquisitions, trades, and contract negotiations. Earlier, we described even more of the duties of the GM, but at the end of the day, their job is to produce winning.

Building a winning team is accomplished by establishing contracts for players that, in turn, result in a product that fans want to see, and those contracts are cemented in writing.

Society today is filled with people who love to win and who love watching winners. These people demand that their sports teams be set up for the best chance to win. The responsibility to provide these teams to the fans falls on the owners. Fans will come to the ballparks when they are confident that their teams are going to do well.

Fans of Major League Baseball (MLB) teams come to the ballpark to see some of their favorite players on the field. It is the responsibility of the owner and General Manager to provide these players to their fans. This is accomplished by drawing up contracts for each player so that the players will be compensated for bringing the fans to the ballpark.

The role of a General Manager is to sign, trade, release, and contract with players and staff involved within the organization.

A team's contract budget is usually allocated by the owners. The General Manager has to spend that budget in the most effective way possible. A budget may or may not offer the financial flexibility to spend in the free agent market. Another way to optimize spending is to go with younger, less expensive players to fill out the roster. Each team has to determine when it is in the club's best interest to sign a player to a long-term deal, all within the constraints of the budget. Players are commonly contracted with long-term deals in the free agent market. Some players are contracted or re-contracted as a result of arbitration of contracts between players and owners.

In any contract consideration, GMs must account for player performance, past and potential, as well as myriad factors that will influence the value and length of a contract. GMs consider

things like character, health, calculated potential, competitive players at the same position, age, position, makeup, market conditions, team budgets, consistency of play and even fan response. Different GMs consider and weigh factors differently, but the result hoped for and contracted for is for a player to have the ability to produce on the field consistently and to win for the fans.

The establishment of Major League Baseball's 1976 Collective Bargaining Agreement (CBA) was the springboard for baseball salaries to skyrocket.

Free agency, salary arbitration and larger draftee contracts created more of the agent/GM throughout all professional sports. GM, agent, and player relations and interactions have evolved since the creation of the reserve clause in that collective bargaining agreement and are vital and essential to establishing the foundation for each club today.

It's interesting to see how salary levels are set, especially with the advent of exploding salaries with today's free agents. GMs have to pay close attention to and be cognizant of other teams' contract negotiations in baseball.

Once a salary level is set for a player with a certain level of performance and years in the game, similar players will want and negotiate for a similar salary. This is one contributing force to the meteoric rise in salaries. This also contributes to more arbitration cases. The owners'/GMs' hopes are to establish and provide player benchmarks along the way.

Mark Shapiro —the President and CEO of the Toronto Blue Jays of Major League Baseball at the time of this writing— has a history of managing incentive-laden contracts. More and more players and GMs are working on performance bonuses that reward players who reach certain achievable, measurable, statistical plateaus or earn league awards.

Without performance or incentive bonuses, some teams have to pay a higher guaranteed salary to the players. This is part of the overall risk calculation for each contract.

All in all, general managers have to consider flexibility, length of contracts, development, competitive levels, and absolute dollar amounts.

In summary, teams need to balance their budget at the end of the day for all working results on the field that will attract fans to their ballpark. Failing to do so results in teams not meeting their goals, whether financial or winning-related.

MLB is a business with profits in mind. To make profits and have the best team possible, a team wants to create a large fan base at and outside the games and use that fanbase to generate revenue and profits. General managers negotiating the right contracts to do this are the most successful.

Jim Bowden, former general manager of the Cincinnati Reds and Washington Nationals, has been quite involved with negotiating player contracts, as any General Manager would be. He has negotiated many contracts with many different agents, with one of particular note, Scott Boras. Scott is considered one of, if not the top, best sports agents.

Jim has offered a few points about his contract negotiations with Boras. Baseball General Managers face this with many of the agents they negotiate player contracts with. This is just one perspective.

Like many other agents approaching the General Manager, Scott Boras first assesses the market by talking to all General Managers, scouting directors and sometimes owners. He communicates his expectations and thoughts on the value of certain players. The value he speaks of is more a comparative value with other players, not dollars and cents at this point. For drafted players, the commissioner's office provides all 30 clubs with a recommended slotting system for each selection in the first few rounds. He will set his own comparative value for players not part of the draft.

For players in the draft he might represent, he looks at a depth chart up and down the organization, from the minor leagues to the major leagues. This helps with assessing the supply and demand of players and the market. Throughout all of this, he always points out leverage points, alternative offers, and plans that a player might exercise.

He advises his clients, much like General Managers advise players, on the most professional way to handle the negotiations, the ball club, media, and fans for public relations.

Boras is ready to negotiate when each ball club is ready. He is very responsive and well-prepared.

Jim Bowden states, "There is not an agent in baseball more prepared for contract negotiations."

He has a team of researchers with all the necessary data. All leading to the best deal, which is at the end of the negotiating and contracting process.

Many do not know Boras is a former baseball player playing for the Cardinals and Cubs as an infielder (he never made it above Double-A). He is also a very smart lawyer with vast knowledge of the markets he works within. Combine all that, and General Managers are usually faced with a tough opponent. Boras loves to negotiate. He's not afraid to bluff. He's not afraid to walk away.

This is not all about Scott Boras, but it puts into perspective what a General Manager faces during player contract negotiations.

An agent's job is to land the biggest contract for his or her client. A team's job is to field the most competitive team at the most economical price. When a player turns out to be a bust or financial albatross, the GM does not do their job.

MLB teams go out of their way to land the players they want and end up blaming the players and their agents when the contracts do not work out. Sometimes, it's pure player performance, and sometimes, it's a burdensome contract.

Here are two things a GM should understand when entering into any kind of contract negotiation with agents and players. Agents know these and practice them. General managers ought to do them as well.

1. Know the Statistical Performance of a Player.

One of the beautiful things about baseball is its rich history of data: home runs, RBIs, on-base percentage, slugging percentage, ERA, saves, and so on.

2. Understand a Player's Value.

A player and agent will communicate their value not in a way that was tied to one season but in a larger, forward-looking way as if their best years were yet to come. General managers prefer, and agents and players know this, that they emphasize long-term value in the right way, which is always more powerful and pleasing than making demands.

It is not easy for baseball executives to balance negotiating a lower financial worth of a player with the need and method to maintain that player's motivation and self-confidence. For example, in salary arbitrations, players will know exactly how much others think they're worth. GMs need to balance a potential player's perception of being on a losing end and motivation to give his all. After all, the GM mindset is that career progression is more important than any short-term payoff or rental situation.

General Managers are, more and more today, faced with decisions related to longer-term player contracts. Much thought has to be given to a contract for a 30-year-old player and how productive they will be for the life of a contract. It's more of taking a chance than a contract for a draft pick or newer player. Some are good, and some are not.

MLB contracts are fully guaranteed, and many include creative financial components like deferred payments. You read often about teams that keep paying players long after they have left the game and/or retired. That's a risk or consideration for all long-term player contracts. The General Manager hopes that none of these long-term, larger big-contracts don't turn into lost gambles.

These contracts usually happen with free agents. Some teams continue to add more bad contracts to player rosters with players that don't produce to the expectations that justified a larger contract. Other GMs have been more prudent and careful when handing out and negotiating deals. Some GMs will elect to pick up the "bad" contracts and have better luck. You hear often that a change of scenery works for some players.

Why does the phenomenon of overinflated, longer-term contracts exist and keep coming in baseball? It boils down to supply and demand.

Signing a superstar player is an investment. That player becomes the centerpiece of your roster, the foundation of your team. There are many returns on that.

An elite player sells tickets. The higher the attendance, the more merchandise a team sells. This, in turn, becomes a negotiating point when dealing with broadcast networks and other revenue generation methods a team gets involved with.

Some GMs are rational about future value. The case in point was when the Cardinals tried to re-sign free agent, Albert Pujols. He wanted more, and St. Louis said they were at their limit. Pujols went on to sign with the Angels (before eventually coming back for a farewell tour with the Cardinals). The Cardinals negotiated without dealing with false future value.

Derek Jeter was directly responsible for generating revenues for the Yankees that were 2–3 times the cost of his contract each year. Elite players equal profits in many cases.

For a GM, there are many angles to successfully land a contract. Some players get unheard-of perks, bonuses, and deferred payments as part of contracts and more.

Ethan Trex of Mental Floss (sourced from *Cot's Baseball Contracts*) wrote about Charlie Kerfeld's Tasty Bonus:

"After 1986, Kerfeld needed a new contract. Kerfeld asked for $110,037.37, matching his number

37 jersey. He also asked for and received 37 boxes of orange Jell-O in the deal. The Astros would soon regret this delicious bonus, as Kerfeld, who was famously caught eating ribs in the dugout that season, would battle weight and injury problems and get sent down to the minors."

Trex went on to report that in 2009, The Boston Red Sox signed starting pitcher John Lackey to a 5-year, $82.5 million deal. Lackey was 31 at the time. Signing pitchers to long-term contracts is risky in and of itself. Pitchers get injured more regularly than position players. The Red Sox built in an insurance clause to help avert this risk. If Lackey missed any significant time due to surgery on a pre-existing elbow injury during the first five years of the contract, the Red Sox would gain a club option for the 2015 season in which Lackey would have to pitch for the Major League minimum salary. That took a creative General Manager. That creative GM was none other than Theo Epstein.

In 1984, General Manager John Schuerholz offered George Brett real estate to get him to the point of an agreement.

Brett was offered a 1,100-apartment complex as "a nice little kicker," owned by Royals co-owner Avron Fogelman. That real estate resulted in a guaranteed cash flow of $1 million from the development.

Roy Oswalt of the Houston Astros received a unique toy incentive in his 2005 contract.

Astros owner Drayton McLane promised to make Oswalt's goal of owning a bulldozer come true if they made it to the World Series. Owner McLane was then held true to his promise in the form of a Caterpillar D6N XL bulldozer for Oswalt. Oswalt ended up signing a required addendum to his contract, a "bulldozer clause," authorizing the club to give him his new toy.

After the 1998 season, Kevin Brown of the Los Angeles Dodgers received, in his contract, a guarantee of twelve round-trip private jet trips from L.A. to his hometown in Macon, Georgia.

Other GM creativity for player contracts consists of bonus clauses, sometimes tied to incentives and sometimes not, deferred payments, no-trade clauses, performance awards, and others ranging from access to a private jet and suites on the road to college tuition.

In negotiating today's exorbitant salaries, GMs are always looking for creative ways to reach agreements without pumping up an already inflated figure. When a GM completes a contract, he has a player. Completed contracts lead to completed rosters. That's always a GM's goal.

Chapter 9: Salary Arbitration — One Necessary Evil

In talking with various GMs, past and present, they are all quick to go through a litany of job responsibilities: player acquisition, trades, free agency, hiring and firing, drafts, scouting, player development and arbitration. There is more, but one responsibility that is somewhat glossed over is arbitration. In the baseball world, the world of a GM and players' arbitration is considered a necessary evil. We will touch on it briefly here since it's on the GM to-do list.

Salary arbitration was instituted as part of the collective bargaining agreement between the Major League Baseball Players Association (MLBPA) and Major League Baseball (MLB) in the early 1970s. The purpose was to provide a system for players not yet eligible for free agency to be compensated based on a comparison with others of the same competence and skills. At the time, it was viewed as a compromise system.

There are different qualifications for arbitrations. Essentially, it is for players who have accumulated a certain number of service days. For more about these, consult SABR.org.

The arbitration process enables clubs to retain control of players, while the advantage to the players is that they receive salaries that are influenced by the market and their own performance. There is a strong desire and benefit to both sides in that the process is designed to promote a settlement of salaries without a hearing. If a case goes to a hearing, the arbitrators must award either the player's request for worth or what the club thinks the player is worth. In arbitration rules, there's nothing in between. That means that there is a risk for both sides to go to an arbitration hearing. In recent years, over 90% of the cases filed have settled prior to a hearing.

January is typically a month of contract negotiations and arbitration for a General Manager. During this month, a player (or usually his agent) and his club each submit a salary figure to arbitration. These figures are given to a three-person arbitration panel of professional arbitrators who are used to hearing diametrically opposing viewpoints. The actual arbitration hearing is then scheduled for early February. Call any general Manager in February, and chances are they are wrapped up in arbitration preparation and hearings.

The way the actual process works, and the one that each General Manager or his designate prepares for, is that each party has one hour to present its case to the arbitration panel, followed by 30 minutes for rebuttal. Present at the hearing is the three-person panel: the player (some represent themselves), his agent, and a club representative, sometimes the General Manager and sometimes someone else within the organization.

After player and team presentations, the arbitration panel decides which salary figure to award. It is an all-or-nothing situation. Players know this. Teams know this. The arbitration panel will choose the proposed figure from the player or the team. As mentioned, there is no middle ground or compromise.

That's typically the method and mechanics of arbitration. Aside from the mechanics, there are all the other intangible considerations of arbitration.

The player is required to be in attendance and listen to the presentation of each side's case. A team, in all honesty and to the point, will try to minimize that player's accomplishments, past performance and future value to the team. At the end of the arbitration process, that same team still manages a player with an intent of dedication to the next season. That is sometimes tough to do after minimizing a player.

In anything related to salary, General Managers must consider their total budget and how salaries relate to that. When General Managers stack arbitration cases, there is a gamble with budget plans before rosters are set.

General managers like to have players signed to contracts before resorting to an arbitration hearing. Many players and teams settle their salaries and contracts before arbitration hearings. It is much better to try and resolve contract differences before a hearing takes place. In most cases, a one-year salary or an extension can be agreed upon before the arbitration deadline.

One intangible point of the arbitration process is that it can be detrimental to both the short-term and long-term relationship between the club and the player.

It's one thing for a player or his agent and a team to negotiate back and forth on a contract, discussing pros and cons in an attempt to settle on a salary number. If a player has to sit in a hearing and listen to the team try to convince an arbitration panel that a player is not worth as much as they think, there is a risk that the process can be disconcerting.

The key that's easier said than done is for neither side to take the trading of barbs personally.

Mike Hazen of the Arizona Diamondbacks has an interesting approach to arbitration. Some of the following come from Steve Gilbert, @SteveGilbertMLB, of MLB:

Mike Hazen has a method, or call it a routine, where he sits down after an arbitration hearing with the player that was just in an arbitration hearing room. When the D-backs win the hearing, the player is usually disappointed. Anyone would be when asking for more money and not getting it. Mike's goal is to make sure the air stays clear.

Hazen calls the meeting with a player the day after the arbitration process ends —accountability. Accountability is one of Hazen's standards for his whole organization. This includes holding himself accountable.

Mike Hazen, as General Manager, attends his arbitration hearings. Things remain very cordial, and players like that, even though it is a rarity for the General Manager to always be present. Each GM talked to had their own philosophy and approach.

One player reported to Hazen that there were no hard feelings whatsoever after a hearing, as the player knew what he was signing up for before the hearing. This same player stated that he felt like the low amount was a good offer and that there was a chance for him to win more. He mentioned he would take that bet every time.

In this case, there were tough presentations on both sides. One point of importance is that character issues weren't discussed or attacked.

As expected, they took numbers and presented them in a way that made the player look worse than he felt. Both sides stretch the limits. The arbitration panel then offers their decision, and both player and team move on from that.

Hazen's approach, deliberation, openness, and fairness make arbitration a win/win for both sides in the Diamondbacks case.

Players and the team also view the whole arbitration process as simply part of the business of baseball.

Trey Mancini, currently a free agent and formerly with the Baltimore Orioles, Houston Astros and Chicago Cubs, had interesting but very honest comments about his arbitration experience. This comes from the York Dispatch during his negotiations with the Baltimore Orioles:

"I'm maybe slightly surprised that we didn't come to a deal, but at the same time, it's part of the process. There's a lot of guys going to hearings, and that's the way the business works. There are no hard feelings or real emotions, I think, that should be attached to it. It's part of the game and part of the arbitration process. It's in place for a reason."

Mike Elias, at the time, had to consider economically how an arbitration decision would impact Baltimore's clubhouse, payroll, and other intangible factors. Elias described arbitration as "mind-numbing.

As a General Manager, he stated, "I'm put in a position where I've got to manage the long-term future of the club, make business decisions on behalf of the club, so there's some natural times when you're at odds over things."

The bottom line for GMs is that they must be prepared for salary arbitration and determine what may be the best course of action (arbitration or settlement) based on the player, resources, time, and expertise.

Arbitration is what it sounds like. It's one more general management task; however, it does take a lot of preparation. It's a good thing it's separate and only 1-2 months in play.

Chapter 10: Ned Colletti — A Lasting GM Fingerprint

When talking to a former baseball manager who has served over 40 years as a baseball executive, you can bet and believe they have seen it all. They have seen it all in baseball and many other things in life. That's Ned Colletti.

If you (or others) are looking for a baseball General Manager who has a background of almost every experience in Major League Baseball, is a four-time Emmy Award-winning baseball analyst, and is a professor of Sports Administration, Negotiations and General Management, all you need to do is look up Ned Colletti.

Back in his days, as General Managers traded seats, roles and teams, anytime a team needed a General Manager, Ned Colletti's name was more than likely thrown into the hat.

Ned Colletti was General Manager of the Dodgers for nine years and has a record of plenty of important general management decisions. Colletti was the Assistant General Manager of the San Francisco Giants before moving to the Los Angeles Dodgers. While with the Dodgers, which was from

2005 to 2014, Colleti had the highest winning percentage of any General Manager in the National League.

General Managers complete trades, negotiate contracts, make offers, are active in the free agent markets and much more as you are learning. In Colletti's case, he did all this and built or helped build teams that qualified for the postseason many times.

Much like other General Managers we talked to, Ned Colletti wants to give back. Besides his many charities, he is involved in and serves as a mentor for several community groups, and he teaches at Pepperdine University. One of the classes the University offers, taught by Colletti, is a class simply called *The General Manager*. He extends this with teachings on the subject of negotiation. Many of his stories and experiences revolve around that key general management component.

Part of the duties of a General Manager, and perhaps the paramount duty, is to be an effective negotiator and communicator. Like many General Managers, Colletti is considered a good negotiator and communicator. Some of this is from his early days with the Cubs, where he represented them in arbitration hearings with the negotiation of player contracts.

Colletti was heavily involved in player negotiations, including working out a contract for Barry Bonds.

His best lesson in negotiations is negotiating for one of his own contracts with owner Frank McCourt of the Dodgers.

On a mid-November day, after hours of talking and tests along the way, the two agreed that Ned did OK and was ready to proceed to more nitty gritty. A salary was offered close to the deadline. Ned knew what his predecessor had made. He also knew his predecessor had a 5-year contract, and these negotiations were happening in year two. If the predecessor was fired, the predecessor would still be paid 3 years of the remaining 5-year contract. Ned was offered a salary less than his 2-year failed predecessor and fewer years.

In the spirit of negotiation, Ned stood up, shook hands, and politely stated, "Thanks for the offer, but you have the wrong guy."

That was a fact, but in the back of Ned's mind, it was a point of negotiation. McCourt asked if he was turning down the offer of being the General Manager of the Dodgers.

Ned said, "Yes. You're offering me less than my predecessor, who was not doing his job and who he decided to replace."

Ned said again that he had the wrong guy as he already had a good job. McCourt then asked what it would take. Ned asked for more money and a longer contract. The deadline, because of Major League rules, was quickly approaching. McCourt finally said he'd do the deal, but then a discussion ensued on an option year.

When Ned first said no, he knew the situation and the many factors of the situation, knew the dire need, and responded. In his mind, he was negotiating with leverage at that point. Ned says you have to have leverage. You have to understand your surroundings and know your situation. Ned knew he had leverage. Ned and Frank made a deal. Ned's Dodger general management career had its starting point and was off and running. According to Ned, there was lots of work to be done and now. Negotiations are a large part of a General Manager's job. General Managers need to have those same negotiation skills when negotiating player contracts. A General Manager puts his fingerprints on a team. Even after a GM leaves a team, players develop and have great successes. Looking back, you can see where certain GMs were instrumental in the beginning of that now baseball star.

That was the beginning; then there was an end. There were times after Ned's departure that people on the team and in the business stated that Colletti is still with the Dodgers, meaning his fingerprint lives on. He is an integral part of the Dodger's team history. His enduring presence is a reminder of how his teams were built and the vision of the future.

We are trying to see the finer points and day-to-day of baseball general management here. Talking with and reading about Colletti and all the ways of his managing produces what really is like a baseball General Manager primer.

Different General Managers work with players, player development and team development in different ways. One of the things Colleti did best was to convince players to push themselves. He sold his players on their potential greatness. That part of the winning recipe allowed his teams to make five playoff appearances during a nine-year tenure.

For any General Manager about to take the helm, here are few Colleti actions to take a lesson from. For fans who want to pull back the curtain and see the inner workings of baseball General Management, read on.

Justin Turner was signed as a minor-league free agent by Colletti in February 2014 and blossomed into an All-Star. Turner was offered a minor league deal instead of a straight shot to the major league roster due to his somewhat failing knees that showed up in his physical exam. Colletti asked him to bet on himself.

Colletti told him, "You're my guy. I know you can play man-to-man. You are making this team. It's just a matter of your health."

Turner recalls: "Ned has been so great, so encouraging, a great baseball mind. I no doubt owe him a lot of credit for taking a chance on me."

This is how Colletti worked. This is what Colletti did best. He convinced his players to push themselves.

Clayton Kershaw, Cory Seager and Cody Bellinger were also drafted during Colletti's regime.

Many would say that drafting those players was an easy part of the General Manager's job. They see talent and make picks. Obviously, there is more to it than that. Having foresight of talent is key. Take the case of Kenly Jansen. Jansen was signed as a catcher from the island of Curacao. Colletti noticed his struggles early on, mostly batting. His development was not panning out. Colletti then convinced his staff, internally, to give him at pitching. That is exactly what Colletti did. He then had the job of getting player Jansen to buy into that move. Jansen pushed back against the concept in the beginning.

Colletti said, "He didn't want to move, but I told him, 'I don't see you as a big-league hitter, I don't see it happening; being a pitcher is your best chance to get to the big leagues. He finally saw what we saw."

Things worked out very nicely, to say the least, as Kenley Jansen is the all-time saves leader for the Dodgers and has turned into a dominant reliever in all of baseball, a true general management success story.

Successes are great, but a baseball General Manager's job does incur stress and much criticism. When a team is doing great, the GM gets all the praise, but if the team is underperforming, they get all the blame. After his GM tenure, the Dodgers gave Colletti the role of advisor, which meant that he still is active with the team, but it relieves the stress and criticism that come with being a GM. Colletti states that an adviser's role still lets him do what he loves and do it in a more relaxed way.

Colletti worked as an analyst on the Dodger's SportsNet LA studio shows and has been involved as a professional scout with the San Jose Sharks hockey team, focusing on scouting at the American Hockey League (@TheAHL) and the National Hockey League (@NHL) levels. I only mention it here because it highlights a significant general manager characteristic. That characteristic is talent evaluation.

"Ned has an extensive background working in professional sports and talent evaluation, and he brings a fresh perspective to the San Jose organization's evaluation process," said Doug Wilson, who was the Sharks' General Manager at the time.

Colletti consistently stood out in the number of players promoted from within his farm system to the show. That is considered short-term value, and only six General Managers in history produced more total short-term value from their farm systems than Colletti.

Ned Colletti's story is just another example of baseball general management and what he once told former Los Angeles Dodgers owner, Frank McCourt:

"The season is like a kaleidoscope. Every day it changes one degree, and the picture is different."

Chapter 11: Nick Krall — Cincinnati Reds — Follow the Path

Cincinnati Reds' General Manager, Nick Krall, has had an interesting path to his position as General Manager. It's interesting, but all General Managers have an interesting yet different path to their jobs. Nick's is worth writing a book about. Oh, wait! It's at least worth including his path in a book on baseball's General Manager jobs and managing the show.

To learn more about this path, you have to look no further than the local paper for Nick's hometown. In York, Pennsylvania, that paper is The York Dispatch. The York Dispatch describes and lays out his path as follows:

In high school, he wasn't a standout player.

In college, he failed in his bid as a walk-on.

In the pros, one of his first jobs was as a part-time bat boy.

None of that, however, deterred Nick Krall from fulfilling a life-long goal.

The 1995 York Catholic High School graduate landed his dream job with a Major League Baseball organization when he was promoted to General Manager of the Cincinnati Reds. Yes, there were a few other baseball jobs along the way on Nick's path, including interning, scouting and operations, logical steps in many baseball General Manager's careers.

In his failed bid as a walk-on at Louisiana State University, in his senior season, he was one of the last walk-ons cut from the team. That team went on to win the national title without Nick.

Now, he is the General Manager of the Reds, and as often said, the rest is history.

When Nick Krall first started in his General Management job, he reported to the then President of baseball operations, Dick Williams. Dick left the ball club, and now Nick runs the whole show for owner Bob Castellini.

Krall's viewpoint and optimistic viewpoint in 2018, as a new General Manager, was about the same as it is in 2023 as a more seasoned General Manager:

"We have a top-10 farm system and some kids who are getting close to being pretty good players," Krall said.

"… We need to make some tweaks, but we're not as far away as folks think."

That's still Krall's mantra today.

Krall's response when people ask him about his goals is the same as that of most General Managers.

"It's winning a World Series," Krall states.

He follows that when others push back and question his dreams with, "…sometimes dreams do come true."

Because of his background in major league scouting, he pays particular attention to this area as it's a primary general management responsibility. He's still a professed learner in the scouting area. There are 8000 players at all levels of baseball. The managers and directors at all levels talk about players, who they have and have not seen, and understand why some like a particular player and others don't. It's a constant learning exercise, and it never stops. Like many components of baseball club and general management, scouting never stops. Nick is in constant conversation with his scouts about prospects, projections, needs and potential fits.

Nick Krall, as well as any other General Manager, directs and has a great influence on The Show. The media has many ways to grade player performance. They also have many ways to grade a General Manager's performance, in other words, the performance of The Show. Here is one set of grading criteria that is a good summation of General Manager responsibilities and has been applied to Krall's recent performance of a more than exciting series of events and season play. These criteria come from Fansided.com, one of the fastest-growing networks of fandom-focused sports, entertainment, and lifestyle sites on the Internet. Notice on each of these how each falls under true General Manager responsibilities:

A team's front office impacts that team's performance and eventual standing in five ways.

Those five are:

1. By the impact of players it acquires from other teams via trade, purchase, or waiver claim. (TRADE)

2. By the impact of players it surrenders to other teams in those same transactions. (CUTS/RELEASES)

3. By the impact of players it signs at free agency or extends. (FREE AGENTS)

4. By the impact of players it loses to free agency or releases. (LOST SIGNINGS)

5. By the impact of players it promotes from its own farm system. (WELCOME TO THE SHOW)

Nick says what almost every other General Manager says about his daily duties:

"Every day is different. You never know what opportunities arise, what players need attention, what crisis needs to be handled and more."

He comes to his office every day at 9:00 am and starts with the mindset of building the best organization for the future.

Nick preferred to describe his duties season by season instead of day by day. Starting in the offseason, he is strategizing and figuring out what his team looks like for the upcoming year. At the same time, he is managing staffing opportunities and issues to put the right organization in place for the team's goals.

He then goes into what he described as "roster cleanup." This includes figuring out and putting in place what has to be done to build up the roster for the next season. Many, including Nick, classify this as the projections of players and rosters for the future. That season he described is the first month or two on the timeline. He then moves to free agency and trades, followed by preparation for the draft.

Spring training soon follows, with his planned and set roster to bring to training camp. The obvious happens during spring training aside from practice and preparation for play. That is a time to evaluate the total roster and choose the best 26 men to bring forward to begin the season. The season starts, and he and others in the organization simply watch players play. Evaluation continues at this point. Not only is all this going on at the major league levels, but similar activity happens at the minor league levels. Player development, what players are moving up and down, and more happens simultaneously with season play.

The other stage requiring the General Manager's time and oversight is the draft stage, along with international player signing. All in all, he takes his season in stages. The more we talked, the more he lumped a lot of his activity and oversight in the same breath: What part of the organization does what, interacting with his internal directors like the director of scouting, international scouts, player development staff, analytics staff, and budget management.

Nick interacts with all his direct reports often. He goes to all the affiliates at least once a year. He makes trips to Arizona when the team plays there as it gives him the opportunity to stop by the Red's spring training facility, which also acts as a developmental facility year-round. His travels also take him to the Dominican Republic and other international venues. One thing he made clear at this point was that scouting and development are the backbone of what the team does and which he is involved in every day.

His direction is that being a small market team, he has to build from within with a player pipeline put together by scouting and player development.

Little did we both know that a few days after our interview, as Nick Krall went about his everyday duties, major league players popped up on waivers whom Nick ended up being interested in. Cincinnati was in the middle of contention for a playoff spot. Nick went into action and acquired two major offensive players to help with the team's push. He tried for pitching help but got beat out by others in the waiver watch who ranked higher for acquisition; just another day in the life of a General Manager. This was not planned nor expected the day we spoke, just a few days before. Nick proved that you never know what opportunities might arise.

Spending time on trades is not where he spends the largest amount of his time. He might also be involved in free agency, staff hiring, manager meetings and more. I asked if he had a to-do list, and he responded by saying his staff managers have more of the to-do list he relies on most.

Nick has a solid background in scouting. He cites that his pro scouting director does a great job. He has regular meetings with pro scouts at the end of the season. During the time we spoke (August 2023), he said scouts were preparing for the offseason, visiting AAA clubs, and preparing for minor league free agency.

More about Nick's daily duties and job responsibilities:

Asking Nick what his favorite part of his General Manager's job was, he was quick to talk about the people: people in the organization, players, and others outside of the organization that he interacts with regularly. Because of his path and previous work, he can be seen talking to groundskeepers and other workers producing the product for the fans.

Nick started and has been involved in the intern program for the team. Many of these interns have gone on to other clubs in promoted positions. He touches base with them as much as he can while visiting other teams. He states that people make the job fun.

He finishes this with, "This is a job — there are only 30 of them — so you aspire for it. But, at the same time, I'd rather win a World Series. That's my goal. That's everybody's goal in sports. That's why we all take these jobs. The scouts and the player development staff, the front office staff, that's what we're here for."

Nick talked about the importance of the MLB draft. The draft is a prime avenue for him and his team to obtain affordable talent and build the team's farm system. After the draft, the process begins to get contracts completed with as many players as possible and to get their pro career started at the team's developmental facilities, which are mostly the same as spring training facilities, and then, hopefully, for the more successful players, the Minor Leagues. He considers the draft as the backbone of the club, the main artery to bring new players to the organization. He knows and has seen first-round draftees becoming immediate impact players.

Under Krall's leadership, the Reds have focused on the draft as a primary mechanism for selecting and developing promising prospects. They have sought to bolster their organization with talented players who can contribute to the team's success in the long term, consistent with their mission of long-term sustainability.

Nick talked about eliminating peaks and valleys and building consistency. He talked a lot about the pipeline.

Charlie Goldsmith of the Cincinnati Enquirer reported from Nick, "We need to figure out how to continue to build through our player pipeline, player development, and scouting. That's got to be the base of everything we do. If that's the base, that's how we'll build long-term success and sustainable success."

A conversation with him confirmed this.

Nick continues to state that the team has to make sure that everything that can possibly be done is being done, from the draft to signing and acquiring quality players, while continuing to put players in that pipeline. Those are the players with the most potential to get to the big leagues. They'll be the players used in trades, in the big leagues, and who are going to do everything they need to do to get to the postseason.

The Dayton Daily News reported Nick's feelings about player development in 2023.

He stated, "I'm proud of the staff as a whole," Krall said, "I'm most proud of how players have developed over the last year. Watching players on this team, you see Elly De La Cruz come from international scouting, Matt McLain and Andrew Abbott, both in the '21 draft from our amateur scouting, Spencer Steer from pro scouting, and Alex Young, a minor league free agent. We've had a lot of guys come through player development or come into our system through scouting. The big-league coaching staff and what they've done with these players to put them in the best position to succeed, the players themselves to just continue to learn and work and fight to move forward, I think the whole process has really impressed me. I couldn't ask for a better group from top to bottom."

That's music to a General Manager's ears.

Just because the time leading up to the trade deadline is what instigated this research and book, I asked him what things were like leading up to that deadline. He said, as one can imagine, that activity during this period of the season is non-stop. Starting in June, he starts making calls to other GMs to see where other teams stand and what their strategies might be. Trade conversations are all about relationships. Part of this is staying in touch throughout the year on an ongoing basis. This approaches July 1st, where not only is he preparing for the deadline 30 days away, but during this time, he starts draft planning meetings with the All-Star break right in the middle. Coming out of the All-Star game week, the phone calls increase, and activity ramps up to make trade deadline trades. More serious conversations are happening, and trades are planned and worked out.

Throughout the conversation regarding the trade deadline, a few key points related to Nick's approach and strategies came out. He is big on giving younger players a place to play with lots of playing. Certain players have to play every day. This is true at all levels. He is careful about bringing in a new player that displaces that playing time with a key player. He is always thinking about the organization's long-term health, not one-and-done players. Rentals sometimes take away from the playing time of developmental players. He sounded like a broken record talking about playing time and development. That's his strategy for the organization, all under his leadership.

Lastly, when discussing the General Manager title and position vs. Director of baseball operations title and job, he pointed out that those are just titles. There needs to be one person clearly in charge. He is the person in charge and reports to the owner of the club. The owner relies on Nick to manage the club and make the necessary decisions.

After talking with Nick, it was clear he was in charge, was passionate about his job and team, and facilitated that with the right people. Nick is clearly a General Manager.

Chapter 12: Bill Schmidt — Colorado Rockies —Managing a Business Surrounded by Passion

When talking to Bill Schmidt, you, right away, get a no-nonsense, get-to-the-point conversation. That's another way to say that Bill is all business. *Baseball* is certainly a sport, but it is also a *business,* and the General Manager is in charge of that business. Bill states that loud and clear.

Even though he has stated that baseball is a business, he is still passionate about baseball as a sport. When Schmidt was asked if working in baseball had always been his goal, he had a very much to-the-point answer.

"It was. It was a hobby at first, but it was more to be a high school baseball coach. Then, I started coaching at the junior college level. Then the goal was to become a major college baseball coach."

Bill Schmidt, a long-time Colorado Rockies front office staffer, was appointed Senior Vice President and General Manager of the Colorado Rockies on Oct. 2nd, 2021.

Schmidt originally joined the Rockies on Oct. 1st,1999, and led the Rockies scouting department over the next 20-plus years as the Vice President of scouting, a position he was appointed to on Jan. 2nd, 2007, and had before his appointment as General Manager.

It had been some time since we talked after his appointment, so I asked him what his favorite part of the General Manager's job was.

He was quick to say, "I like baseball."

That was all he needed to say. That passion was on display the whole time I talked with him. He likes the fact that he gets to put together a team, a team with a common mission that is also passionate about baseball.

Upon taking over the Rockies, Schmidt was faced with a long journey ahead of him to rebuild a struggling franchise. His job soon became one of filling holes and making improvements on the roster.

Schmidt came to the General Manages job with over 30 years of scouting experience. He proudly states that with a scouting background, you get experience. You have to have a work ethic and a love for the game, which are all essential for a General

Manager. By the way, his scouting played an integral role in the selection of many key players. A few players of note that reflect are Troy Tulowitzki, Charlie Blackmon, and Nolan Arenado.

Since officially gaining the title, Schmidt has solidly been building up the Rockies roster with player contract extensions and free agent contracts in a way that a head scout wishes for, but can't make the ultimate decisions like a General Manager.

Bill Schmidt talks a lot about the people around him in just about any subject we have explored.

When asked about his appointment as GM of the Rockies, he expressed, "It meant a lot that Rockies Owner Dick Monfort and Chief Operating Officer Greg Feasel had confidence in me to fill the role. I felt good for the people around me because, again, it's not all about me. It's about a group of people, and they trust that we can get the thing going in the right direction."

He had this to say about the people and how they relate to his stated direction for the team: "We have a belief that we think is strong, and if you ask anybody inside our organization, they will tell you the direction we're going. We might not be up on top of the mountains screaming it out, but we know what direction we're heading in."

He has also stated that one of his primary tasks for the organization was to improve communication inside the offices at Rockies' headquarters. As Schmidt put it, "Get everybody pulling on the rope in the same direction. Not only the players but the whole organization."

Upon Schmidt's appointment as General Manager, MLB reported that he said, "There's a lot of good people, first and foremost, that are involved with the Colorado Rockies, so we've just got to get back to the process where there's trust and communication." Again, a tremendous people orientation, all in the job of a General Manager.

Bill said he had the ability to bring a group of people together. It comes down to trusting your people and building a team. That's general management at its finest.

As expected, after talking to several General Managers, Bill Schmidt's response to the question of what a workday looks like for him was the same as others: it's different every day. The workday, however, changes depending on what season they are in. He also stated that there is spring training, pre-season, regular season, post-season, and off-season. He talked of his duties as part of the whole organization's effort, department by department, function by function. He was proud of the organization he set up, overseen by him, the General Manager. This is where he also brought in the business side of the sport. Different people are responsible for different things, baseball-related or business-related. Budgets were a topic related to the business side here.

Regarding team management, an MLB GM oversees the entire coaching staff and department managers and allocates resources within a budget set by the team's owner. A GM is expected to make strategic and tactical decisions that will lead to a successful team on the field. Within a budget from the team owner, the GM must make decisions on player contracts, coaching salaries, draft expenditures, and other expenses to ensure financial sustainability. Simply put, that is the business side of baseball and more of a General Manager's responsibility.

The conversation with Bill kept coming back to his mission of finding opportunities to improve the ball club. This includes always watching the waiver wire, paying attention to trades, negotiating with free agents, the draft, and more. One thing he pointed out was when he brings young guys into the system; he wants them to get as much playing time as possible.

This is at any and all levels. That mission is very clear to the entire organization as they work to improve the ball club.

The conversation moved to trades, specifically deadline trades. Due to his conversation with other General Managers, he usually knows which players other teams are interested in, especially during the time leading up to the trade deadline. This gets matched up with whether his strategy is buying or selling during this time. He mentioned that strategy is dictated by the obvious: what are the needs and gaps, what is in stock to trade, and what do others want? It boils down to a supply and demand balance.

In somewhat of a selling mode, he used the trade deadline period to move a couple of relief pitchers and a few position players. He knew what other organizations wanted, he knew his gaps, and the job, at that point, for buyer and seller is to find a fit. Sometimes, that fit is all metrics related, and sometimes, it's a fit of the intangibles a player brings or offers. Related to those intangibles, you hear things like, "He is a good clubhouse guy," or, "He has playoff experience." The intangibles can sometimes be the most important part of a trade.

All of this trade discussion happens between General Managers, but sometimes Assistant General

Managers talk to other Assistant General Managers, doing the majority of the legwork for trades. This conversation is not necessarily impromptu, as Bill stays in touch with many General Managers (not all 30) all season long.

Another common thread between General Managers that Bill emphasized is the intact relationships that allow these conversations and trades to happen when it is time. He has his favorites and is closer to some GMs than others. The peak of relationship building through conversations occurs during the General Manager meetings and the winter meetings, where all General Managers gather together in the same place at the same time.

Bill Schmidt emphasizes building a foundation for his team. This involves acquiring the right players and talent and waiting on them as they develop in their time frame. Sure, he has players that he calls place holders until the younger players are ready, but he is always looking to advance the organization from that foundation. Ultimately, with each step of the way, his goal always remains for the organization and players to get better.

Schmidt says, "We are always going to be a draft, sign, and developed organization. That's who we are."

Regardless of what we talked about, there were common themes: always trying to create a better organization, a passion for the sport, and producing a product that the fans enjoy. Just mentioning that baseball is a product for the fans shows his balance of the sport and the fact that it is also a business.

To sum up, Bill Schmidt works passionately in a sport that he loves while at the same time respecting that it is a business and it takes a whole lot of people to move it all ahead, all under his supervision and direction. The entire personality and execution of the organization starts at the top.

Chapter 13: Bob Howsam — Putting "Manager" in General Manager

Many past General Managers have their own legacies and accomplishments to learn from. While we can't focus on all of them, Bob Howsam is one of those who is worth focusing on.

Talks with past and present baseball General Managers reveal different approaches, strategies, and tactics, all with different results. Focusing on one General Manager of the past, Bob Howsam, shows many general management fundamentals in action and lessons to learn, more than many other GMs. It is worth reviewing his life and work as a General Manager.

Bob Howsam's actions and accomplishments were spread throughout the sports world of the 1960s and 1970s. During his 11 years (1967–77) as General Manager, "The Big Red Machine" captured six division titles from 1970 to 1979, four NLCS titles, and two World Series championships in 1975 and 1976. Howsam's work as the Cincinnati Reds' General Manager will be remembered as his masterpiece. His efforts in building the Big Red Machine took a good team and turned it into a legendary one.

The Reds had been purchased by a group of local businessmen who bought the club primarily to keep it in Cincinnati. They did not know anything about baseball team management. In view of that, they hired Howsam and gave him a three-year contract, more money, and complete power.

Unlike most GMs at that time and even now, Howsam ran the entire operation in Cincinnati with very little interference from his owners and bosses. He even represented his owners at baseball's owner meetings. He wasn't an owner but acted like he was and took the management of his team to heart.

While he was known as the engineer of The Big Red Machine, he was known among the industry as one who understood the General Manager's role and organized and operated accordingly.

Fundamentally, Howsam pointed out that the key to any successful business operation is outstanding personnel who are productive, well-trained, and dedicated employees. These qualities were prevalent when looking at his success as a General Manager. Besides, Howsam, with his brilliant organizational skills, put together a team of people he trusted, people he listened to, and people whose opinions and advice he valued. When listening to those opinions, he didn't mind disagreement. He encouraged people to challenge ideas. However, the final decision on anything material was always his.

All this started with Howsam when he was allowed to set up the organization as he saw fit. This included reorganizing the front office. He added new staff, increased advertising, and enhanced sales, all responsibilities of a baseball General Manager. Howsam himself said that running the Reds was anything but a one-man operation. His organization and re-organization reflected that.

Howsam depended on them to tell him the truth. It was the fundamental basis of the organization.

Also reported by the authors of "In Pursuit of Pennants," Howsam was clear when he said, "Yes men do you no good," he continued, "The rule I had was say what you want, I may not agree with you, but say it. But when you go out that door, don't you ever talk about how that isn't the way you would have done it. We're a team, and once we decide what we want to do, nobody's going to second-guess it, or you won't be around long."

In the book "In Pursuit of Pennants: Baseball Operations from Deadfall to Moneybag," authors

Mark Armour and Daniel Levitt point out that Howsam not only expected his staff to thoroughly know the players in his own Reds organization, but he also required that they know all the other teams and their farm systems as well or better than the teams themselves did.

For example, he would ask his people: What do the Phillies need? What do the Astros need? What players do they undervalue? Which up-and-coming players are blocked from advancement? These questions and answers allowed him to be strategic when talking with fellow General Managers.

He often knew as much about what another team needed as they did. He also knew where they had too many players in a particular position. He approached these conversations with the identity that the Reds could help solve the problems and fill the gaps of other teams. Howsam truly created and fed a culture of baseball intelligence and organizational excellence.

Much of the Bob Howsam information is sourced from Armour and Levitt's book, "In Pursuit of Pennants - Baseball Operations from Deadball to Moneybag."

Howsam was considered a master dealmaker. That deal-making was backed by an organization of talent evaluators. He had full trust in their abilities and formed a communication system that was second to none. With an amateur draft and no free agency, the GMs of the time had to rely on scouting, talent evaluation, and their own instinct, expertise, and wisdom.

In the era before free agency, General Managers like Howsam were often judged on their ability to make stellar trades. At the time, that was the best avenue for improving a club roster.

As an example, every fall, he held multi-day meetings to review, in detail, every player in his organization. He did the same for players in other team's organizations. He required his staff's frank assessments of his team and asked for detailed information on how players on other teams might be valued by their management. When he called a GM to make a deal, he wanted to know before dialing the phone what players the person he was calling (usually a fellow GM) undervalued.

Early in Howsam's tenure, Red's President, Francis Dale, stated that he was impressed by the thoroughness of Howsam and his staff.

He said, "Bob could go to a General Manager, like the Astros General Manager (Spec Richardson at the time), and talk with great respect. It was not unusual for Howsam to approach a General Manager and point-blank state, 'I've studied and analyzed your team, and here are my reports on what your team needs. What your team needs is this, and so on.' And so, he convinced a team about what they needed that he was then able to say, 'I just happen to have what you need.'" It was general management at its finest.

Bob Howsam redefined the word "Manager" in baseball general management. He ran the business side as well as the baseball side with efficiency and great effectiveness. His work is a lesson for any General Manager working towards a championship goal.

Chapter 14: Trades — Acquiring Players and Building Rosters

Fred Claire, former Los Angeles Dodgers General Manager, states in his writings, especially in his book "Extra Innings," and during our conversations, that baseball trades have changed dramatically through the years.

He is quick to point out that General Managers are judged by trades they have made. Fans love to play the "General Manager role" in their minds and judge the trades. Many times, fans judge trades after the fact; after a player proves himself or not. General managers don't have that foresight, which is a fan's hindsight. Regardless, trades are a part of the game and what fans attach themselves to. That adds to the interest of the game.

General Managers are the architects of trades. Trades are made to improve the team. This is done during the offseason up to around August 1st, which is known as the Trade Deadline. But more on the whole trade deadline saga later.

Free agency is part of today's trades. Free agency is a subject in and of itself that is complex and sometimes complicated for a General Manager to make a trade.

Today, more and more information is available to the average fan, especially for General Managers, on online sites, streaming news and games, blogs, rumor sites, and many media reports. All of this allows fans to discuss trades that should or shouldn't have been made. It is way more than the days of young kids trading baseball cards as if they were players. Fans like to play the General Manager. Fans always have a better idea of how to improve a team. Fans have opinions on baseball trades. If only General Managers would listen to them all (impossible).

Trades today are not like baseball trades in the days of old. Today, teams, staff, and General Managers aren't completing trades on the back of a bar napkin at their favorite pub. Today, they are inundated with things like endless data, email communication back and forth, texts, cell phones, astronomical salaries, arbitration clauses, and players to be named later, all leading to contracts of all shapes and sizes, all lengths and dollar amounts, no trade contracts, and the fear of losing players to the free agent market at the end of their contract (that is traded for).

General Managers used to meet each other and talk at events like the All-Star Game and World Series. There used to be hospitality suites set up for all to meet and talk. Key staff were also present. Today, that has all been overrun by sponsors and sponsor suites. GMs have resorted to texts and email messages. Trading is different today.

There are many variables in a baseball trade. Every trade is different for many of the mentioned factors.

Even with all of the changes talked about here, baseball is still baseball. The game is still the game. There are still 3 outs to a half-inning, 9 innings to a regulation game, no time limits on the game, and the game is decided by a winning score. Baseball is still baseball.

Any player can be traded if they are under contract. Trading can happen from the day after the end of the World Series through July, usually by July 31st or August 1st, by any major league team. GMs are always trading or have trades on their minds as well as on their to-do lists. Looking at past years, agreements with agents and players were simple. Don't laugh at the back of the napkin approach. It happened. Teams just agreed on which players they'd like to trade. Today, it's more complicated (see above), takes more time, and can lead to confusion for General Managers and players, not to mention fan understanding.

The late Bing Devine was a long-time General Manager of the St. Louis Cardinals and New York Mets. Bing had a process for making trades. He explained the process in his book "The Memoirs of Bing Devine."

"You win some, you lose some…and sometimes you get lucky," he wrote, "But you don't get lucky if you don't take the chance."

He finished this by outlining his "four tricks" for a trade.

1. "You've got to need the player.

2. You've got to have good reports from your scouts and talent evaluators.

3. You've got to have the guts to make the deal.

4. You've got to get lucky. But if you never have the guts to do anything, you'll never get lucky. You'll never give yourself the chance to be lucky."

Today, all four tricks continue to be in play for all GMs, either in this form or a modified version of their own tricks.

Also, today, there are many more people on both sides involved in a trade, a lot more compared to the days when General Managers would shake hands and make a deal.

In the old days, two General Managers would state their needs to one another. If they had players that fit each other's needs, a trade could and would be made. Neither had to consult with any others. That's how deals and trades were made: General Manager to General Manager. Today, because of the plethora of people involved and the methods of communication, trades are not as personable as they once were. However, General Managers are still in charge.

Today, you still hear General Managers say that they make trades primarily to fill voids or gaps in their present teams. They may have an excess of players in particular positions that are appealing and complementary to other General Managers, which is the foundation of a trade.

True today, economic considerations are more and more in play for each and every deal and every trade.

Scouts are the eyes and ears of the team. They live and die by the many statistics of the sport. General Managers take information from the eyes, ears, and statistics as part of evaluating a potential trade. Other factors considered are the team's basic needs, whether pitcher or position player, and whether there are too many players for one position on the team. You will continually hear talk of scouts, whether in trade discussions, draft discussions, or international players.

Our General Manager acquaintance, Fred Claire, former Los Angeles Dodgers GM, stated a few years ago (which still holds true today) that trading is part of the evolution of the game.

The role of the General Manager and the structure of the process related to trades are much more sophisticated. The days of trades made at the bar are gone. Throughout the 70s, the game was changed dramatically. And teams have changed in a like manner.

Fred stated, "I think that we in baseball and in life really have to deal with what is."

Today's "what is" is different from yesterday's "what is."

For more on all of this and things like the details and background of the reserve clause, arbitration, free agency, agents, specific trades, odd trades, and more, I refer you to the book, "Going, Going, Gone! The Art of the Trade in Major League Baseball" by Fran Zimniuch.

Making a trade to help your team and the opposing team is one thing. Most General Managers are careful of their integrity. They would never send a player to another team with knowledge of ill health, controversies, or illegalities present.

"The word of the General Manager about the health of the players is the most essential part of any deal," said Fred Claire.

"It is your credibility and your word that is on the line. Good deals are deals that work and work for both clubs. As a GM, your credibility is so important because you need the trust of the other teams."

Teams are permitted to trade only players currently under contract. Unlike the NBA, NFL, and the NHL, draft picks are not tradable. Trades between two or more major-league teams may freely occur at any time during a window that opens two days after the starting date of the final game of the World Series and closes at the specified time on the date specified for the MLB trade deadline.

In many trade deals, you will often hear of a "player to be named later." Usually, that is code for a minor-league player. Sometimes, teams cannot immediately agree on a specific player at the time of a trade, and sometimes, it's a question of when a player is eligible to be traded. That's when you hear and see the player to be named later. In these cases, the player to be named later must be named within six months. Cash or some other consideration may be exchanged in lieu of the player to be named later if one can't be determined in time.

As an example of a player to be named later or, in this case, something that might happen later, in 1994, the Minnesota Twins traded Dave Winfield to the Cleveland Indians (Guardians) right at the trade deadline in July of that year. One of the conditions of the trade was a player to be named later. The player to be named in the trade would be a Double-A player. The league was on strike, with the rest of the season and number of games played in question. If the strike was resolved and anywhere from one to 15 games were played, the player to be named later would be a Class-A player in return. If no more games were played, then as part of the trade, the Indians' (Guardians) General Manager at the time, John Hart, must write a check for $100 made out to the

Minnesota Twins and take Andy MacPhail out to dinner.

There were no more games played in 1994 as a result of the strike (which ended the day before the start of the 1995 season). It never came out where Hart and MacPhail dined together.

There have been thousands of trades in the history of Major League Baseball, some noteworthy and others changing the entire baseball and team landscape. Many of these trades involve superstars of the day dealt for up-and-coming hot prospects in a team's system. Sometimes, the deal works out for both sides, and sometimes, the trade is a bust.

Depending on what side of the trade you are on, trades are successful and contribute to a General Manager's goals; sometimes, they are a bust. Here are some that can be classified as momentous or a bust if you are on the wrong side of the trade. "Momentous" can be defined differently depending on how anyone looks at a trade.

The following may be classified as some of those momentous trades:

1. The trade that was talked about as one of the biggest trades in baseball, and the best for one side, is a trade involving Babe Ruth. In the trade,

Babe Ruth was traded to the New York Yankees, and the Boston Red Sox received $125,000. At the time, it wasn't momentous or the best for Ruth as he didn't become the historic hitter he was until he joined the Yankees (after the trade). He went on to win four World Series titles and hit 659 of his 714 lifetime home runs. From that trade came the Curse of the Bambino. Boston wouldn't win a World Series until 86 years after that trade.

2. One more trade worth noting is a 1954 trade between the New York Yankees and Baltimore Orioles. Eighteen players were involved. You don't hear of that size of a trade today. That was one of the largest deals in MLB history. Baltimore sent Bob Turley, Don Larsen, and Billy Hunter to New York for Harry Byrd, Jim McDonald, Hal Smith, Gus Triandos, Gene Woodling, and Willie Miranda. The deal was completed on December 1st of that year when Baltimore traded Dick Kryhoski, Mike Blyzka, Darrell Johnson, and Jim Fridley to New York for Bill Miller, Kal Segrist, Don Leppert, Ted Del Guercio, and a player to be named later (which apparently never occurred).

General Managers have goals; they have to pay attention and have to think about Bing Devine's four tricks. They also have to be creative. George Weiss, General Manager of the New York Yankees in 1954, and Arthur Ehlers and Paul Richards, co-General Managers of the Baltimore Orioles at that time, got very creative.

Much is written about the impact on players and families when a trade is made. The fact that players are traded or moved is not always easy on a GM. Sometimes, this involves releasing a player, demoting them to the minor leagues, and out trades. Players are loyal to their teams and the organization that acquired and backed them. Many times, a GM and his team will share this same loyalty.

Thinking back on the conversation I had with Nick Krall of the Cincinnati Reds, I asked him who communicates to a player that they have been traded. Nick was clear and said that when his team makes a move, the Manager and a front office person will typically sit down with the player to be traded or sent down. He likes to have two people present to ensure that the player involved knows any and all the reasons and details why the move is happening. Nick is typically that front office person. He stated that he always wants that to be the case except when he is traveling and on the road.

This same approach is how Fred Claire, former GM of the Los Angeles Dodgers, communicated trades. Fred was adamant that he didn't want any player to hear about a trade from anyone but him. Ninety-five percent of the time, Fred communicated directly to the player. Exceptions were if travel schedules didn't align. That wasn't often, as Fred Claire traveled with his team and traveled on about 75% of the team's road trips.

The trade deadline can be an incredibly difficult time for players. They realize baseball is a business, and they have little or no control over their professional futures. Players don't like hearing their names coming up in media reports while playing or on social media conversations. Sometimes, those rumored trades happen, and sometimes, they don't.

A potential trade means to a ball player that they might be transferring their entire life to another city quickly, even the next day. Sometimes, that even means playing for a new team the next day. Players have families and the moving process to think about. It can be highly disruptive on many fronts.

At this time, minor-leaguers get to see the business side of the game for the first time and how it can affect them, especially if their name is linked to a deal and they suddenly recognize that the club they signed with first may not be their team for much longer.

MLB reported communication of these trades on the day after the trade deadline.

The day after the 2023 trade deadline, MLB reported how the Cleveland Guardians handled communication of trades to the players involved. Guardians President of Baseball Operations Chris Antonetti and General Manager Mike Chernoff had a strong desire to be in Houston at Minute Maid Park on the Wednesday before the trade deadline. Three of Cleveland's players who had played important roles in the clubhouse, even some that had subpar performances, were traded to new teams right before the trade deadline.

MLB reported that Antonetti and Chernoff always preferred to be with their team, delivering trade news alongside manager Terry Francona in his office instead of over a phone call. The trade deadline activity happening at the front office in Cleveland also required their presence. It was a tough choice, but staying back and working on trade deals made it impossible for them to be in Houston with the team.

Antonetti said at the time, "It's a really hard balance. In an ideal world, we would've been able to be at the game with the team, but we couldn't be in two places at once."

They opted to show up the following day.

Antonetti and Chernoff wanted and knew they needed to at least be present as soon as possible to be available to talk with their team. Mandy Bell, reporting for MLB, stated in her report that baseball is a business, and players understand that, but that doesn't mean that decisions made by the front office never trickle into gameplay. The Cleveland executives made a trip to the team because they wanted to make sure they did what they could to prevent any effect on play.

Antonetti said, "We're always cognizant of the message our trades send to the team any time, especially around trade deadline time. Any moves with players coming and going can potentially be disruptive. So, what we try to do is stay connected with the field manager, the coaches, the clubhouse, and the team as much as we can, and if we do make trades, be around to talk with people about it, whether that's players or coaches or staff just to talk through it."

One more thing from our General Manager extraordinaire, Fred Claire, formerly of the L.A. Dodgers, is how he worked with his field manager on all trades. Fred stated that in all the trades he did, the manager was always involved and consulted. He never made a trade without getting input from others: mostly the manager involved, other coaches, major league scouts, and even minor league scouts. You never know who might know something that might be important in the trade or deal.

As you have seen, the trade deadline period is a very dynamic period in the life of a baseball General Manager. Executing trades involves at least two teams and two General Managers working together toward what everyone hopes is a win-win situation. The General Manager is the architect of the trade. The "perfect trade" eventually turns out to benefit each team, which isn't lopsided for one team, is not always easy, takes "give and take," and sometimes —really many times— takes creativity. The goal is always for each General Manager to accomplish his goals of improving the team on the way to the ultimate goal of winning.

Chapter 15: MLB Scouting — A GM Essential

Through 1964, the New York Yankees captured 29 pennants and 20 World Series championships. One of the ingredients that makes something like that happen in the major league baseball world is good players.

In talking to the various General Managers, most of them talk about how best to acquire good players. Those avenues are free agency, the amateur draft, trades, the Rule 5 draft, Latin American free agents, and more. Each of these is only as good as the organization is good at recognizing talent.

In the early New York Yankees' heyday, they assembled a renowned team of scouts who, in conjunction with the most professional General Manager and front office administration, delivered a consistent stream of baseball's top prospects and players.

When you look at the Yankees' scouting success, it comes down to two primary components: Organizational and administrative. The team built an efficient and effective organization. This meant that scouting was seen as a priority, and everyone knew that. It also meant that there was a sound strategic direction for the team and organization. The Yankees made sure to give their scouts the tools and resources they needed to succeed. After that, the team hired some of the greatest baseball scouts and set their mission to actively engage in finding and signing the nation's best baseball prospects. **Source:** Daniel R. Levitt, author of several award-winning books, including *Paths to Glory: How Great Baseball Teams Got That Way* (2003, with Mark Armour).

That's how 20 World Series championships are won. That's what scouting does for an organization.

Ask any General Manager what it takes to build a successful roster and minor league system, and you will immediately get the answer: scouting. One of the reasons you get that answer immediately is because many General Managers —today and of the past— came up through the ranks of scouting.

Fred Claire says that one of the biggest parts of time management for a General Manager is being good at delegation. This was the case with Fred and the scouting staff. He was very involved with hiring scouts, and was blessed to have a top-notch group.

On the professional side, Fred maintained daily contact with his scouting department. The amateur is just as important but much more vast. At that point,

Fred talks about putting complete trust in the scouting director. Trusting in people who are dedicated to their job, traveling all over, and passionate about the sport are all qualities that come with the scouting staff.

With the responsibility given to his scouting staff comes respect for their suggested picks at draft time and trades. He listens openly and may challenge but rarely goes against his scouts' recommendations.

Baseball scouts travel across the country (and internationally) to watch and evaluate baseball players to determine if players' talents and skills qualify them to work for the organization the scout represents. There is so much information today available on MLB scouting. Information gets to be more in-depth and voluminous every year. Our attempt here is to tie scouting as an important component of club management to the role of the General Manager.

Let's start with just a little background and base information on scouting. According to the Indeed.com career guide, Baseball scouts typically work for sports organizations that draft and hire professional baseball players for minor and major league teams. The responsibilities of a baseball scout can vary depending on the organization they work for, but there are several common duties these professionals perform no matter where they work:

- Traveling to various locations, including high schools, colleges, universities, and other countries, to watch baseball games.

- Observing and analyzing players' skills, abilities, and talents to evaluate players' fit for the organization they represent.

- Coordinating with players to recruit, counsel and provide additional advice on the steps players can take to earn a place on a team.

- Observing, critiquing, and assessing players' abilities during games to determine if their skills match what the organization is looking for.

- Collecting and organizing information about schools, players, and their locations.

- Scheduling appointments and meetings with schools, team coaches, and players.

In all of the conversations with the various General Managers, scouting always comes up as a key component to building a team and eventual success. Scouting and drafting functions fall under the responsibility of the General Manager, including international scouting and development. Many, if not most, of the General Managers surveyed have some background in scouting. Scouting is a good base for a General Manager and is obviously a key asset in structuring a team's roster and makeup.

When you have a General Manager like Ben Cherington, who has a background in scouting, you have a greater probability of picking the right players, building the right roster, and succeeding.

Many General Managers began their baseball path as scouts. Cherington was one of those beginning his professional baseball career with the Cleveland Indians as an advance scout in 1998 and joining the Red Sox organization in 1999 as a Mid-Atlantic area scout. From there, he became a baseball Operations Assistant. Cherington's other roles include Boston's Coordinator of international scouting, Assistant Director of player development, and Director of player development.

Cherington understands scouting. Cherington understands player development, and all that bodes well when acquiring players and building rosters.

Dana Brown, now General Manager of the Houston Astros, like many other GMs, came up through the scouting ranks. Brown played minor league ball with the Phillies before transitioning to a job in the scouting department. As he rose through those ranks, his accomplishments included drafting more than 40 big-leaguers and seven All-Stars.

General Managers oftentimes get major credit for the superstars emerging from a team's system, but credit should really be due to the scouts in the organization.

Just take a look at the scouting background and resume points of just a few of today's General Managers. Notice how many times scouting and player development are mentioned:

Alex Anthopoulos – General Manager - Atlanta Braves

- Scouting Department In-office Coordinator, Florida Marlins
- Area Scout, Marlins
- Scouting Coordinator, Toronto Blue Jays

Ben Cherington – General Manager - Pittsburgh Pirates

- Area Scout, Boston Red Sox
- Baseball Operations Assistant, Red Sox
- Coordinator of International Scouting, Red Sox
- Assistant Director of Player Development, Red Sox
- Director of Player Development, Red Sox

A.J. Preller – General Manager - San Diego Padres

- Scouting Department, Los Angeles Dodgers
- Director of International Scouting, Texas Rangers
- Director of Player Personnel, Rangers
- Senior Director of Player Personnel, Rangers

Brian Sabean – former General Manager of the San Francisco Giants

- Director of Player Development, New York Yankees
- Scouting Director, Yankees
- Vice President, Player Development and Scouting, Yankees
- Senior Vice President, Player Personnel – San Francisco Giants

- Assistant General Manager, VP of Scouting/Player Personnel – Giants

These are just a few. There are many more.

There was a time when the best way to become a General Manager in the Major Leagues was to play as long as you could, followed by taking everything learned from the travels, the games, the players and coaches, and the minor league journey to then become a scout.

Nick Krall, General Manager of the Cincinnati Reds, stated that his team had many players come through player development or into his system through scouting. It doesn't get any more important than this to a General Manager.

Roland Hemond (1929-2021), a recipient of the National Baseball Hall of Fame's Buck O'Neil Lifetime Achievement Award in 2011 and a longtime SABR member, has talked about how fortunate he was to have enjoyed more than 60 years in baseball. Having been in the game since 1951, he realized and has stated that organizations will fail without competent scouts who possess the ability to not only sign players but also project the eventual development of their candidates. He went on to talk about how the baseball world would not have prospered without scouts. Everyone in baseball, and fans all over the world, must not forget the scouts and should shower them with praise and recognition.

The understatement is that General Managers rely very much on the scouting and player development roles. General Managers can't see all the players, and if they do, it might be for one or two games or at-bats.

Lou Gorman (1929 – 2011), who worked with scouts for over 30 years and was a former Farm Director for the Orioles and Royals, Director of player development with Kansas City, and GM or Assistant GM with the Mariners, Mets, and Red Sox and executive scout with many, many years of experience and stories, stated in an interview before his passing, "I don't think you could ever get away from having good scouts. You don't win without good scouts. A General Manager can't see every player. Nobody can. It's impossible. GMs have to rely upon a scout's judgment on players."

Lou went on to say, "If I go out and look at a player for two games and I've got a scout that's seen him for 10 or 15 games, and he likes him, I'd better stick with the scout's judgment over mine."

Before his passing, Lou Gorman told one story in his interview with Bill Nowlin, A former VP with

SABR and author of many books on the Boston Red Sox, that is worth noting here.

I'll quote it as Lou said it so I don't miss anything: "I'm in the office the next Wednesday. It's about 2:15. In comes this kid from Arizona State. 18 years old. He's on the football team as a freshman, on a football scholarship. He says, 'Hi, my name is Reggie Jackson.' I said, 'Mr. Young tells me you can play baseball.' He says, 'Yeah, I can play baseball.' So, I bring him into the clubhouse. Paul Blair calls him over and says, 'Come on, kid. We'll get you dressed for the workout.' Reggie, at that time, had power. He had speed. He can throw. He can do it all. I'm awed by him. The regular guys come in about 4:30. Charlie Lau. Gene Woodling. They're by the batting cage watching. He's hitting them into the bullpen. Line drive in the upper deck at the stadium. So Lau says to me, 'Where's this kid play in the system?' I said, 'Charlie, he's a freshman in college. He isn't signed.' He said, 'Lock the gates. Don't let him out. You'd better sign him.'"

Mark Feinsand, reporting for MLB, asked Bill Schmidt, and he later confirmed much of this when I interviewed Bill, "With Amateur scouting such an overwhelming task, how do you keep track of so many amateurs and make sure you aren't missing anyone?"

Schmidt's response, speaking as a very experienced and seasoned scout, stated that no one can see everybody, every prospect and player that may be available. That doesn't mean he didn't try to see everybody, but he couldn't. It physically is not possible. In all of my discussions with Bill Schmidt, he always emphasized people who made up his staff, people he met in the business along the way, and players and prospects he met in all his years as a scout.

When Schmidt was named the General Manager of the Rockies, he once again emphasized the people.

Upon his announcement, he said, "I felt good for the people around me because, again, it's not all about me. It's about a group of people, and they trust that we can get the thing going in the right direction."

This emphasis on the "people" continues in his discussion of scouting. He clearly stated that you have to trust the people all around you. It comes back to the process of scouting, player development, and team operation.

The old adage about scouting is you can't "dabble" with it. Scouting is a year-round job during all seasons. It's a matter of attending many events and games in the summer. Sometimes, the best competition he sees is during the summer. That is especially true for kids and prospects from the northern, cooler parts of the country.

Schmidt stated, "With scouting, you're trying to see as many at-bats because I can see them in April or May in upper Michigan or upstate New York or New England, and I don't know what I'm going to get. You try to do that during the summer."

Scouting gets players to the big leagues. Schmidt shared this from his acquaintance Dave Garcia, a coach with Colorado's Buddy Bell.

Garcia said, "It's not hard to get to the big leagues because people put you in the big leagues. It's hard to *stay* in the big leagues."

Schmidt elaborated and said the percentage of guys that can stay in the big leagues for longer than three years becomes really small.

One last note: at the time of the writing of this book, during a matinee day game in Detroit with the Cincinnati Reds, Chris Welch, TV broadcaster for the Reds, pointed out as relief pitcher Sam Moll took the mound. Reds' General Manager Nick Krall probably didn't expect the kind of performance that

Moll was delivering since he had arrived from a trade with the Oakland Athletics.

While he was quick to credit Krall, he cited Moll's contribution to the Reds' team as another outstanding performance by the Reds scouts. It was the only trade the Reds pulled off at the 2023 trade deadline, and it was paying off.

Chapter 16: Player Development — General Management of People

The foundation of successful MLB clubs is made up of many pillars. One of those pillars is a successful player-development system. Translated, that means a strong minor league system and development activity like spring training. The goal here is to take acquired talent and bring them to a more elite level in on-field performance.

When I talked to General Manager Nick Krall of the Cincinnati Reds, he mentioned scouting every time and coupled that with player development. He referred to his scouting and player development staff many times.

It's often said that scouts find the talent, and player development improves those found. Said another way, player development is a process to help ensure amateur baseball players are prepared for a career at the professional levels of Major League baseball. Without player development, teams will find it difficult to progress to their end goals.

General Managers are charged with investing millions of dollars into the organization in the form of many components, but especially scouting. One of the results of scouting activity is recommendations for the major league draft. Players are then drafted and entered into the organization. It's now up to the team to turn this drafted talent into the players they hope for and their true, realized potential, including improving skills and techniques that a GM expects from a major league professional player.

All MLB teams have staff devoted to scouting as well as player development. It is a major part of every organization. Player development staff are responsible for educating draftees about baseball strategy, team culture and philosophy, strength development, nutritional guidance, and mental health over and above pure baseball player skills.

When Fred Claire was General Manager of the Los Angeles Dodgers, he worked very closely with his player development staff. He did have a person in charge of player development, but he also wanted to be close to AAA managers, AA managers, pitching coaches, and hitting coaches, all knee-deep in player development. Once decisions were made in these areas, with Fred's involvement, operations were turned over to a minor league operations manager.

Fred had phone calls once a week with minor league managers at every level. He wanted to hear directly what the issues and opportunities were for each.

In Fred's terms, he had a farm director responsible for running the farm system. Assisting him were minor league directors and, of course, the director in charge of player development. Fred was good at acquiring talent for his roster. He wanted to be sure that talent continued to grow and feed ongoing rosters.

Here is what a General Manager thinks: How do I balance player development? In other words, I want to be sure that I don't have too many draftees and rookie players with a lack of experience, and I don't want to have too few of those players with the energy and enthusiasm that is needed to excite a set of fans while working towards winning a World Series.

The Los Angeles Dodgers have long been considered the gold standard for player development. Many GMs pattern parts of their own player development after them.

The Dodgers have won nine National League West titles since 2013, capped by a franchise-record 111 season in 2022. The Dodgers have been known to have a top-five farm system, even without high draft picks. Their strategy has been to place players that leave with young, homegrown stars again and again. Homegrown means those that have come through their player development system.

One Dodger rival NL executive stated, "They're hitting on all cylinders. They draft very well. They develop players very well."

The Dodgers have managed to turn prospects and younger, veteran players into instant stars and high performers almost annually. They continue their winning ways while maintaining an endless prospect pipeline. Prospects need to be developed once in the system. They know this and have that system in place. Those in charge of that system report directly to general management.

The Dodgers invest heavily in player development. That is a General Manager directive. That investment provides for the best coaches and the best development professionals. That investment also allows them to provide minor leaguers with the best facilities and things like weight training and nutrition. They consider this to be the foundation for superior physical development as well as skill development.

Player development takes many forms. Will Rhymes, director of player development for the

Dodgers, says, "We get players who are really young, and a lot of times the lowest-hanging fruit is simply helping guys mature physically. Our performance and medical staff are excellent. We feel like we have the best strength and conditioning out there. Combine that with the nutrition (and) a lot of the jumps you see in players from year to year simply comes from being in fantastic shape."

Not to give anything away, but the Dodgers recipe for player development is simple. Baseball America reports that for advanced players on both the pro and amateur sides, through both traditional scouting and analytics-based methods, they make no bones about seeking athletic, versatile players. They look for players who hit for average and have strong plate discipline. Once they find these players, they believe they can teach players how to add power with swing adjustments, assuming contact skills and at-bat quality are already present. The Dodgers look for those ingredients and take players to new levels with swing and at-bat adjustments.

One more quick note that was memorable is when Andy MacPhail became General Manager of the Baltimore Orioles. He really wanted to create, according to him, a "top echelon scouting and development franchise." As it turned out, his farm system appeared to be more efficient at developing pitching. MacPhail's strategy then, in the spirit of player development, evolved to "buy the bats and grow the arms."

In order for this type of player development to work, all players have to be open to change. Finding those types of players circles back to scouts who judge what's in a player's head and their mental makeup.

One common feature of Dodger players in the player development system is that when they transfer to higher leagues, including the major league, they transition smoothly. They don't encounter the same ups and downs that other team's rookies encounter.

The credit for this goes to the culture and communication instilled in the organization. This is what baseball General Managers work hard for.

Matt Beaty, a corner infielder/outfielder who spent parts of five seasons in the Dodgers' system before making his major league debut, was surprised to learn when he got called up that Dodgers trainers, strength and conditioning staff, and hitting coaches already knew his pregame routine after speaking with their counterparts at Triple-A levels and below.

Baseball America reporting on the Dodgers player development: "Communication, information synchronization and player individualization have become hallmarks of the Dodgers organization. The effect has fostered an easy transition for new arrivals, who don't have to worry about deciphering unfamiliar scouting reports or adjusting their pregame routines. They can just go out and play."

A good player development system works with a team with the right culture. The culture of an organization starts at the top with the GM.

Matt Beaty went on to say, "We want coaches who are positive and who exemplify the values we think are important in our players. Creating lifelong learners, really high baseball IQ, people who have tremendous work ethic…That's the environment we want our players to be in."

The General Manager's goal is to do what the Dodgers have done. They have a scouting and development infrastructure in place that continuously develops elite homegrown players.

Baseball American concludes their report with, "They have a young core of superstar talent, a culture and infrastructure that allows players to flourish, and the financial might to make any additions they want."

One rival National League executive said, "The Dodgers have done a very good job of player acquisition, and then they've given their players everything they can think of to help them succeed. That's a tremendous recipe."

Player development doesn't just happen. The proper resources, mindsets, and coaching have to be put in place to go along with a vision and message from the General Manager. That's a General Manager's job.

The Arizona Diamondbacks have done similar things with their own approach mixed in.

Field Manager Torey Louvello tells his organization that the organization believes in development, even at the major league level, to the point that teaching never stops. That is the culture that permeates the whole organization.

Louvello also says, "When we take the field every day, we teach."

Whether the team is in the middle of a pennant race or having a less-than-stellar season, they continue to talk about the future. The coaching staff spends time teaching and especially working with the new and younger players daily.

GMs strive to have the situation Lovullo has. He will state, "The coaching staff has been unbelievable. They do go out there every single day and work their butt off to make these players the best versions of themselves,"

"We do depend on player development (department) in a lot of ways. We know that there's a process that they follow. Once that player passes through player development and is sent up to us, that player development doesn't stop."

It's often mentioned that players talk about putting the work in or working hard. That's a reflection of development.

Player development directors work for the GM. Ryan Garko fills that development role for the Detroit Tigers. As Director of Player Development, he describes his job as being very broad with many details. He has to mix this with his and the organization's long-term vision.

In Tigers' camp this spring, there's a house finally rising from the foundation.

Garko stated, "It started in minicamp, when players worked through a variety of creative drills on a daily basis — pitching machines set up at different angles, three-plate drills to help with timing, pitchers training with core velocity belts, and more."

To the outsider, it's hard to tell which of these drills are helpful and which are more, for example, for show.

But listening to Garko talk, it sure seems the most meaningful work from the Tigers' new player development staffers is happening even further behind the scenes. Coaches are often meeting with players, explaining what the data says about them and how they can improve and optimize their game.

In mini-camp and spring training, players worked through a variety of creative drills on a daily basis — pitching machines set up at different angles, three-plate drills to help with timing, pitchers training with core velocity belts, and more.

Everyone in the organization is getting a new level of baseball education.

Cody Stavenhagen, staff writer covering the Detroit Tigers for The Athletic, reported from the Tigers and Ryan Garko, "The biggest change for some of our young players is there's not a Tigers' pitcher in the system anymore that doesn't understand what they do well, what they don't do well, how to lean into what they do well and help them get better on the other pitches in their arsenal, and pitch usage. We've had so many conversations with pitchers in our system. They just might need to tweak their pitch usage a little bit, and they can take off."

That's the teaching and development throughout the Tigers' system from the top league (major league) to the bottom (rookie leagues).

Former Tigers' Manager A.J.Hinch was known to have said about the Tigers' player development efforts, "It's a huge change culturally. New ideas, people coming from different organizations, and new leadership. There's a ton of energy. And it mirrors a lot of what's happening in the big leagues. That's done by design."

It's valuable in a system like this to have development for things other than raw baseball skills.

Part of international development is providing help away from pure baseball skills to baseball life and life in general as players transition to playing in the US. The Tigers add and emphasize staff members to help players make that transition.

According to Ryan Garko, "It's not just teaching them English, either. It's teaching them how to function in the United States, whether that's how to eat, how to do their taxes, everything, everything they're gonna need to know. We're gonna try to surround those guys with as much support as possible. We put real resources and surround those guys with as much help as we can."

The goal of his player development becomes replenishing talent on an ongoing basis.

The Tigers do emphasize tech and data, but they also spend a lot of time on what they call the human element, which they consider a key part of player development.

After hearing the examples and methods of all of these teams, it becomes clearer that player development is what will separate teams in the future.

Finally, Reboot Motion, a sports biomechanics company helping coaches develop players and improve performance, states that focusing on a data-driven player and player development, in general, becomes more important and easier to implement every day with the right tools and systems. They offer that player development as the single best way to drive value for an MLB organization.

Investing in people is a winning strategy for a General Manager and the team.

Chapter 17: General Management For the Trade Deadline

The trade deadline is probably unlike any other part of a GM's year or job. This one period of time can affect more people in the sport than any other event during a season. Forget routing by trade deadline time. Whatever routine exists, you can bet trade deadline time disrupts that with a bang. There is no choice for a GM, scouts, their staff, or even players but to adapt to that time. It's a part of almost everything, what everyone on the team does or affects activity.

Some describe this time as taking on mythic proportions. Ask anyone involved in making the big decisions during that time how they feel, and they will say it's the best time of the year (unless you are accepting the Commissioner's Trophy for the World Series Championship). It's the point of the year when a GM can readily impact the team at a critical juncture. It is a very exciting time for baseball General Managers.

With the never-ending duties and the many directions a GM is pulled, preparing for trades is one of those tasks that never goes away. It seems that working on trades is happening all the time for a GM. Sometimes, those deals are immediate; some are for the near future, and others are for the next year and beyond. Always studying current rosters and ways to improve is at the forefront of the General Manager's job. With this comes the search for players who can feed that improvement, fill the gaps, and make a better team.

One of those intense periods of time for trades is at and right before the Major League trade deadline. The baseball trade deadline period is a time when teams search the market, burn the phone lines, and work towards finding the perfect piece to lead them to the Commissioner's Trophy at World Series time. The trade deadline puts the General Manager of a team in the middle of the spotlight and even under a magnifying glass.

The "trade deadline date" setting determines a deadline for trading players between teams.

The Trade Deadline is the last point during the season at which players can be traded from one club to another. For instance, the 2023 Trade Deadline was Aug. 1st at 6 p.m. ET. The deadline date is usually right at the end of July or, in this case, the first of August. Per MLB's release last year on the CBA: "The Office of the Commissioner shall have the flexibility to set the Major League Trade Deadline on a date between July 28th and August 3rd."

After the deadline, no more trades. Players can still be moved between teams if they are on waivers and picked up.

Why even have a trade deadline? When you think about it, the purpose of a trade deadline is to keep a competitive balance towards the end of the season. Sometimes, teams are almost at the point of extending into the playoff season. Picking up a player or a few can sometimes fill their needed gaps and propel them to the next level of the season.

Baseball history shows that trades were not allowed at the beginning and didn't happen. In 1901, the two primary leagues at the time, the National League and the American League, established rules permitting trades. There were rules for that then, and throughout history, trading rules have changed often.

The first trade deadline was established by the National League for the 1917 season. Through much thought and reviewing the trading timing and dynamics, the League chose August 20th as the target deadline date. The American League set its first trade deadline in 1920 and picked a date of July 1st.

Both leagues switched deadlines from time to time. For 60 years after 1923, the deadline was June 15th, 1985. In an attempt to resolve a player strike, the deadline date was changed to July 31st, and it has remained that way ever since.

There is ongoing discussion among MLB ownership representatives to possibly change the date. That, as of this writing, remains to be seen.

Steve Phillips, former GM of the New York Mets, describes the time of the trade deadline as an exciting part of a GM's job. He states that as a General Manager, despite feeling "sweaty" leading up to the deadline, it's the fun part of the job and season. He describes that fun as "getting the competitive juices flowing."

The preparation for trade deadline time depends on each team's trade deadline strategy. Trade deadline check-in calls tend not to start until at least May, when teams start putting together their target lists based on both need and availability. General Managers survey which clubs might be in the playoffs and which will not. They scope out which players' teams might be willing to trade based on being a buyer or seller. Time is spent understanding who is entering free agency and who might fill a short-term role. No one knows what surprises will surface at the deadline, but teams will surely have their target lists prepared. This is their deadline roadmap, as each team and each trade is monitored.

Suppose you are one of the clubs that calculate the numbers, look at the standings, and realize you have little or no chance to play in the postseason. In that case, you then have to evaluate those players who are the core of the team for the next year and beyond and look at who might be considered for a trade for something to help the team achieve its future goals. If this is your team, you are probably a seller.

Things move quickly at trade deadline time. The preparation needs to be done and ready for the hundreds of players who might be part of trade talks once the season starts up to the deadline.

During this time, especially the week leading up to the deadline, baseball General Managers are always on the phone, emailing and occupied by the many text messages, communicating with other GMs about possible deals. A busy GM could have 4 or 5 trades or deals going at the same time, all in an attempt to complete before the deadline. Even though teams have star players, the General Manager of an organization is the most important team player at the time of the deadline.

At this time of the season, a General Manager has to decide if his team will be or have a chance to be a post-season contender. If there are thoughts of being that post-season contender, they have to plan, before the trade deadline, how to try and trade for or acquire players that would make immediate, positive impacts in the clubhouse, produce wins, and get to the playoffs. Teams with that strategy and approach are termed buyers. These deals could potentially make for a changed playoff race.

There are many sub-strategies that go into being a buyer at trade deadline time. It's not just all about going after a particular position where you have a gap or need a stronger replacement. Sometimes, it comes down to adding players with experience either in the general playing field or in a playoff atmosphere. Maybe bolstering character on the team, in general, could be an important stabilizing and calming influence.

Dan Evans states that he had that very thing in mind when he traded for Robin Ventura. Dan said he knew Robin well during his Chicago White Sox tenure. He just knew that a player like Robin would improve his Dodger club that was about to go into a postseason but had not been to one in nearly a decade. Dan says Ventura's contribution to the clubhouse was "enormous and immediate."

Making trades will result in new faces in a team's clubhouse, with others saying goodbye to their current club as a result of the trades.

If a General Manager decides his team will not be in contention, they are termed to be a seller. Trying to beef up a roster at this time turns teams into buyers. That's the basic and most elementary way to describe a team at the deadline; however, there are specific strategies that dictate the moves or lack of moves during that time.

Here are a few examples of trade deadline strategies developed by a team's General Manager: some are very specific, and others are less directed, as summarized from 2023 MLB.com reporting. Any of these could easily be on a General Manager's to-do list.

- Be aggressive and find ways to make a current roster click.
- Add pitchers, preferably ones who aren't rentals.
- Reinforce the pitching staff.
- Add a starter, reliever.

- A little bit of this, a little bit of that.
- Bring in some power.
- Acquire as many prospects as possible.
- Trade veteran starters for prospects.
- Add a functional right-handed bat.
- Trade for a starting pitcher or two.
- Little or nothing.
- Decide a path and be decisive.
- Add bullpen help.
- Sell and make room.

The trade deadline strategy directs the GM to trade accordingly. Seeking players to improve the team (buyers) or trading away players that other teams see value in (sellers).

General Managers need to be totally prepared for trade deadline season. Jim Bowden, former Cincinnati Reds and Washington Nationals General Manager, states that preparation begins with scouting your own current players. Some may be part of a trade, and others may be part of a newly beefed-up team. General Managers must have a feel for the value of a hot 17-year-old prospect at the lowest level of the organization just as much as having a feel for an All-Star veteran on the team. Scouting your own players also helps identify gaps, although a season's results to date will generally dictate a trade deadline strategy.

The preparation also involves evaluating the market, other teams' players, and prospects. That's where the scouts come in. Scouts supply GMs with information about players' skill levels, physical tools, general intelligence, baseball intelligence, competitiveness, makeup, character, intangibles, and past and present performance, all leading to a GM's guess on future performance. Along with other teams' player evaluations, a good GM will understand other teams' needs, wants, and trading strategies. This produces the target list of players for trades. Other teams do this same thing, and if they have an interest in a GM's player that he had in his plan, available for trade, then there is a match. A trade is made.

I asked Ben Cherington of the Pittsburgh Pirates what it was like during the week leading up to the trade deadline. He stated that July for his team and probably for all other General Managers is very busy not only because of the trade deadline but it's also the time for the MLB draft.

Ben also stated, "It's a very exciting month full of opportunities to make a difference for the team.

We see a lot of each other in baseball ops during July! Lot of long hours and takeout."

Here is an example of a General Manager in action during the trade deadline. Sometimes, there is success, and sometimes not. Mike Hazen of the Arizona Diamondbacks set as his trade deadline strategy one of needing to start pitching.

12News KPNX in Phoenix, Arizona, reported at the time of the deadline, "It was a challenging deadline for sure given the dynamic between the sellers and the buyers," said Hazen. "My gut tells me that the lack of sellers meant that the buyers were trading with one another, and we didn't want prospects in any of these deals."

Hazen further stated, "I would much rather be coming into a deadline rather than talking about prospects we acquired, but by talking about major league players our fans are going to watch...because I think the first four months of the season have proven that this is an exciting team to watch with talent, and we felt they needed some kind of a jolt, and we hope that we have provided that. "

Another example of a trade deadline strategy is one often stated by Mike Rizzo, General Manager of the Washington Nationals. According to 106.7 FAN, DC's Sports Radio's report, "With the Aug. 1st MLB trade deadline approaching (the date of the 2023 deadline), Washington Nationals General Manager Mike Rizzo is eyeing another chance to improve the rebuild and said, 'we're open for business'." That was his trade deadline strategy, although briefly stated.

Prior to the National's series-opening game at Wrigley Field right before the trade deadline, Rizzo told the assembled media, "We're going to do deals that make sense for us. We have a plan in place, and a blueprint in place for this rebuild. We're always open-minded, and we'll always be aggressive. That's not to say we're going to move everybody. But if we can move the ball forward in the rebuild process, we certainly will be open-minded to it. I think the key word is 'deals that make sense to us.' We're always open for that, no matter what our record is, and this year is no different."

Honestly, this could almost act as a generic strategy for each and every year's trade deadline.

John Perrotto of PittsburghBaseballNow.com reported on Ben Cherington's deadline strategy. At the two-thirds point of the 2023 season, the Pirates and General Manager Ben Cherington determined they were sellers rather than contenders or buyers. They shipped four veteran players to two different teams. Cherington, as General Manager, considered being somewhat neutral and keeping those players. He saw the opportunity, hopefully, a winning opportunity, to get some young talent or access to young talent that they didn't have previously. He also saw a way to open up opportunities for some other players to have a chance to play for the team for a longer period of time. It was a tough strategic decision, especially in view of what they got out of the four veteran players they put up for sale. The organization valued the players as much for their mentoring of young players, advice, talking strategy with younger players, tutoring, and leadership as their play on the field.

When asked about the trades, Cherington remained very appreciative.

He expressed his sentiments: "We acquired all of them this past offseason with the intent to get better," Cherington said. "I shared with all of them my appreciation for them because I do believe we brought them here to help us get better, and I believe we got better, in part because of their contributions on the field and off the field. They did exactly what we hoped all four of them would do. We'll be rooting for them."

It would be a lot better for the organization and fans for the Pirates to reach a point where they are adding players and prospects rather than dismissing them.

When asked what he thought of being a buyer instead of a seller, Cherington said, "For sure, it's a lot more fun.

GM's have a challenge at trade deadline time to focus both on the short-term and the long-term state of the ball club. No one else thinks more about this than the General Manager. Many have inputs, opinions, and suggestions, but a GM must maintain the proper focus at this time.

General Managers are second-guessed about trade deadline decisions all the time. This is especially true when a team comes very close to making the playoffs. That was the case with Nick Krall and the Cincinnati Reds at the close of the 2023 regular season.

Mark Sheldon, MLB reporter for the Cincinnati Reds, talked with Krall about his decisions to make moves or not make moves.

Mark asked Krall, "Could the Reds have made it into October playoff baseball with more help?"

Cincinnati added only one pitcher during the trade deadline period.

As far as not adding more, Krall stated, "I am not second-guessing myself. I don't have any regrets about not doing anything more. I still wouldn't have given up players on our roster for shorter-term assets. You're just robbing Peter to pay Paul, and you're losing years of control with a lot of your younger players. I just didn't think it made any sense."

That's just one reflection of the on-the-spot strategies that have to be decided on at the deadline.

Chapter 18: Analytics — Measuring the Sport

Almost every General Manager interviewed for this book mentioned analytics in one form or another.

Sandy Alderson, former New York Mets General Manager and later President of the team, was the first modern GM to actively work with analytics in managing his team and making team decisions. Now, every team has an analytics effort and a whole department managing research and development, including baseball analytics.

Before Alderson fans attended games, they listened to those attending the game talk about the game and the "should of and could ofs." Batting average and earned run average were talked about, but that's about it. Then, that migrated to a time where calculators, laptops, charts, and spreadsheets took over. The game was managed through myriad numbers, statistics, data, and formulas. Not only was the game being managed with data, but analytics became part of team management and roster decision-making.

Today, if you watch or listen to any game broadcast, you will hear the talk of data and statistics galore. From historical data and comparisons, scorekeeping, performance forecasting, and specific player and team statistics, big data and analytics are now at the forefront of team and player management.

Big data has made its way, not only in team management but now to fans and media people. Analysts, play-by-play commentators, and fans use data constantly. Sometimes, that's in the form of explanations or predicting what may or may not happen. This has also exploded with the advent of the multitude of fantasy leagues. Baseball General Managers are astutely aware of this.

Simply stated, data, statistics and analytics allow teams and General Managers to track performance, forecast and make predictions about a player, and frankly, make smarter decisions on and off the field. Players still make up the team and are the ones who have to execute and win games. Data allows General Managers and coaches to put the right players in place at the right times.

If you want to be convinced that big data is here to stay, just look at the organization chart of each team. Here are just a few titles related to analytics. All of these report upto the General Manager of each team:

Cincinnati Reds: Director of Baseball Analytics, Senior Data Scientist.

Chicago Cubs: Senior Analyst, Research and Development, Analyst, Research and Development, Analyst, Performance Analysis, Analyst, Research and Development, Analyst, Baseball Analytics, Analyst, Baseball Sciences and over 25 more people in their Research and Development department.

Los Angeles Dodgers: Director, Quantitative Analysis, Quantitative Analyst.

New York Yankees: Director, Quantitative Analysis.

Tampa Bay Rays: Lead Analyst, Baseball Research and Development, and over 20 analysts.

Boston Red Sox: Director, Baseball Analytics, Assistant Director, Baseball Analytics & Research Development, Manager, Baseball Analytics and 16 others in the Baseball Research & Development department.

New York Mets: Vice President & Assistant General Manager, Baseball Analytics, Director, Baseball Analytics, Manager, Baseball Research & Development, Manager, Minor League Analytics and way more staff members

Back in the '70s and even into the '80s, a General Manager's duties revolved around managing operating budgets, trading players, and working through arbitration hearings and drafts.

Years later, budgets and arbitration were delegated to those below the GM. General Managers used to sit in smoke-filled bars and talk trades over drinks. That's simply not how it is any longer. The mechanics of trades and club management have become much more sophisticated, backed by data.

The most famous General Manager involved in analytics besides Alderson was Billy Beane. As famously shown in the blockbuster movie Moneyball, the 2002 Oakland Athletics were asked by ownership to cut payroll and try something new. General Manager Billy Beane and his assistant, Paul DePodesta, decided to embark on a new strategy to make decisions on player acquisition. They called it power analytics. Now, the use of data and analysis has expanded league-wide. This widespread use of this new advanced tool has changed baseball and given General Managers a whole other area of responsibility and management.

Arriving in the early 1970s, this new decision-making emphasis was termed sabermetrics. Sabermetrics revised old ways of thinking about player performance, especially when only looking at many of the established statistics such as RBIs, pitchers' won / loss records, and earned run average. It all boiled down to asking whether great players are really great or how *good* is good.

According to Britannica, Sabermetrics aims to quantify baseball players' performances based on objective statistical measurements.

Bill James is a baseball writer, historian, and statistician whose work has been widely influential in the sport. He is often referred to as the father of Sabermetrics as the most influential baseball statistician in history.

As James described, Sabermetrics is "the search for objective knowledge about baseball." James also attempted to expand the thought process beyond the back of a baseball card and into what he called the "ever-expanding line of numerical analysis." Teams no longer want to be bound by conventional wisdom.

General Managers now consider baseball statistics and analysis to predict the performance of players. It gives teams a competitive advantage or in today's world, the ability to keep up with competition that is using data. Sabermetrics helps a team forecast results by making predictions based on statistics and previous data.

Before Sabermetrics, player evaluation was different. Decision-making utilized way fewer metrics. Many talked of baseball from the review of the backs of baseball cards. Batting average, home runs, and RBIs for hitters—and wins, ERA, and strikeouts for pitchers were what one had. That's all that mattered back then. That all matters now, but data-based decision-making offers GMs so much more.

One report stated that we are on the threshold of kids bringing Texas Instruments graphing calculators to the ballpark instead of their gloves while also projecting future exit velocity instead of chasing foul balls.

Michael Fishman, Assistant General Manager and head of the team's analytics department for the Yankees, oversees one of baseball's largest analytics staffs. As reported by Mark Feinsand, MLB.com, Executive Reporter & MLB Network Insider, "As far as The New York Yankees, analytics is part of our process," Fishman said in a previous interview with Joel Sherman of the New York Post.

"It is part of the process for most teams. It is providing information for our decisions, for our players, for our coaches, and for the front office. It is not making all of the decisions. It is part of the decision to make sure we are making good decisions using all of the tools available."

The sport of baseball is ever-changing. Athletes continue to be bigger, stronger, and faster. Adapting and evolving is now a must. The way baseball General Managers draft players and build rosters is causing organizations to explore analytics and how statistical data and analysis will benefit the team. General Managers want to marry objective thinking with subjective opinions, especially from coaches, managers, and scouts.

The Astros won their first World Series after hiring data-driven General Manager Jeffrey Luhnow, who has since left the job. With the information available at the time, he dismantled the team, rearranged what was left and built the rest from the ground up. This included traditional-minded coaches, scouts, and players.

The Chicago Cubs championship in 2016 was attributed to data-driven decisions by President of Baseball Operations, Theo Epstein, and General Manager, Jed Hoyer.

David Stearns, former General Manager of the Milwaukee Brewers and now President of baseball operations for the New York Mets, was described as having the ability to blend the analytical and scouting ends of the operation, translating that into a vision for any team he works with.

Today's General Managers can learn a good lesson from the above-mentioned examples and previous GM actions.

The General Manager's front office staff has grown primarily because of the inundation of information to process. Baseball Research and Analytics departments play a critical and fundamental role in things like player acquisitions, player health and medical information, and what to spend and who to spend on in the free agent market. Data also now drives the first-year player draft and most everything related to the international market.

Baseball is overwhelmed and consumed by analytics now. Statistics have always been a part of baseball within this modern age of technology; data is even more prevalent and used more and more.

Stan Kasten, who presided over 14 division title winners in Atlanta as President, former President of the Washington Nationals, and the current President and part-owner of the Los Angeles Dodgers, told ESPN writer Jerry Crasnick, "Over the last 10 years or so, there's been a tremendous influx of new information that has to be managed. In addition to keeping track of all your players, coaches, and scouts, there's all this new information for every single one of them, so there's a need for more specialization and division of labor than there's ever been. There's clearly a need for more people and systems and hardware and more analysts. Even if you don't like it, your competitors are using it, and you're going to fall behind if you don't."

General Managers must ensure now that they, the manager, and coaches create a culture of respect and trust that allows data, statistics, and analytics to be used and embraced.

Data analytics have made baseball general management and the sport far more interesting. Teams that formerly had less of a chance to win are now competing for championships. Big data and analytics are here to stay.

Chapter 19: Player — GM Relationships and Interactions

Interaction between General Managers and players differs between General Managers and has over time. Some are present in the dugout, on the field - pre-game, and in the locker room post-game. Others are behind the scenes and not as present in front of players, especially with today's emphasis and use of player agents. Player/GM stories are few, but there are some.

Some General Managers talk directly and interact actively with players.

In Moneyball, the book on Billy Beane and the general management of the Oakland Athletics, there is a scene where Billy is talking directly to a player. It didn't take long. It was on the spot in a fleeting moment, but that was Billy's style:

Oakland player Jeremy Giambi was summoned to General Manager Billy Beane's office.

Upon knocking on Billy's office door, he peeked in and asked, "You wanted to see me?"

In his no-nonsense style, Billy said, "Yeah, Jeremy, grab a seat."

Billy then proceeds to tell Jeremy, "Jeremy, you've been traded to the Phillies. This is Ed Wade's number. He's a good guy; he's the GM. He's expecting your call. Buddy will help you with the plane flight. You're a good ballplayer, Jeremy, and we wish you the best."

That line of communication doesn't happen as often today as it did in the days of Moneyball, especially with the involvement of the many agents players are represented by. In this case, it was direct face—to—face communication between the General Manager and the player.

General Managers are involved in player communication in different ways.

Dennis Rasmussen was a tall, left-handed pitcher who pitched for many teams during his MLB career, including the Yankees. Rasmussen tells of the time he was in the middle of direct communication with the team owner, followed by more direct communication with the General Manager.

It was 1986 spring training for the New York Yankees. The Yankees were visiting Pompano Beach, the spring home for the Texas Rangers. Dennis Rasmussen, the Yankees' left-hander, was one of several pitchers scheduled to pitch and be put on display on what was known at the time as Yankees marathon exhibition day.

Lou Piniella was the Yankees' manager. Their strategy that day was to score early and take the pressure off of the pitchers so that they all could get fair evaluations. A fair evaluation was suspected because of swirling, howling, and windy conditions at game time. As a side note, Rasmussen was in a tight competition with teammate Tommy John for the fifth spot in the Yankees' rotation.

Aside from the pitcher evaluations, the wind ended up being a friend of opposing batter Curtis Wilkerson, a hard-hitting infielder of the Texas Rangers. At the wrong time (when is there a right time for an opposition's home run?) Wilkerson unloaded on Rasmussen for a 3-run homerun over the left field wall. That was not part of the Yankees' game plan that day.

As Wilkerson was rounding third to plate his score, Yankees' owner George Steinbrenner, often in the stands at spring training games, stood up as part of a loud crowd and yelled loudly, "That's it. I've seen enough. You're on your way back to Columbus."

Columbus was the location of The Columbus Clippers, a minor league baseball team playing in the

International League and the top Triple-A affiliate of the New York Yankees at the time. Steinbrenner had mentally started to plan Rasmussen's airline ticket to Columbus. You can't get any more direct communication than standing up at a live game and yelling to the player at the top of your lungs.

Rasmussen heard it; his wife and friends in the stands heard it, as did family members, and he hung his head as most would do after giving up a long ball. After the game, reporters quickly got to Rasmussen and told him about Steinbrenner's grandstand performance. All Rasmussen could say was, "I hope I get another chance."

He knew he was on display, under the microscope, and fighting for his future. (He had given up three home runs that day, which produced all of the Rangers' runs in their 5-4 victory over the Yankees).

He later got the opportunity he wished for. A few days after that game, he was called, on a last-minute notice, to pitch against the Kansas City Royals in Ft. Lauderdale, KC's spring training location. Dennis pitched 7 innings and gave up one run and no home runs. The next day, Piniella named Rasmussen the fifth starter.

Little did Dennis know that General Manager Gene Michael had to stand up to owner Steinbrenner to retain Rasmussen. It was more of defending to keep Rasmussen when Piniella wanted Rasmussen as the fifth starter, and like many Yankee decisions, Steinbrenner was in the middle of it. Steinbrenner said no to that, feeling the same thing that happened with Curtis Wilkerson's wind-blown home run would happen again.

Steinbrenner even said, "We can't do that. He's going to do the same thing he did in Pompano."

GM Gene Michael stood up for Rasmussen. The fifth starter decision was held, and Rasmussen went on to be the best Yankees pitcher that year, winning 18 games and losing 6. Michael shares that story often as Rasmussen and fellow players get together through their post-playing years.

Needless to say, Steinbrenner chose a very direct method of player communication, with lots more communication happening between the player and General Manager, Michael, as Michael did his thing. This one action solidified his career, and Rasmussen went on to pitch years after that.

Sometimes, General Managers can make their own decisions, and sometimes, they have to yield to an active owner.

We've already discussed that General Managers and owners all have their own ways. Communication and direct interaction with players can lead to unique management methods between players and top brass.

Herm Winningham was a reserve center fielder who played mostly with the Washington Nationals and the Cincinnati Reds. Herm was part of the 1990 wire-to-wire World Series Championship team with the Cincinnati Reds. Herm took us inside another GM/player interaction.

Bill Stoneman, known better as Stoney, was the General Manager of the Montreal Expos in 1987/1988. Herm was part of that team with regular playing time at a top level.

Early on in 1987, Stoney was hands-on with his players. Some General Managers were, and some weren't. Stoney called Winningham into his office. Players are never sure why they are being called into a manager's office, especially a General Manager's office. Back then, General Managers were more involved in team play and operations than they are today.

In his own management style, Stoneman proposed a deal to player Winningham. Stoney was frustrated with the number of fly balls Winningham was hitting and wanted him to hit line drives in order to utilize Winningham's speed. Line drives instead of fly balls would get him on base and allow Winningham to steal more bases. Stolen bases lead to more runs.

Bill Stoneman's deal with Winningham was shaped like this. For every ground ball Winningham hit, Stoneman would pay Winningham $50. For every fly ball, Winningham would pay Stoneman $50.

After the first month, Winningham had pocketed $600. The second month yielded $1000 more bonus money, growing to $1500 in the third month. Stoneman had accomplished his goal, had created new habits with Winningham, and was at the point of ending the deal. Winningham called this Stoneman's gadget. Winningham said General Managers of that time had many gadgets they used. GMs were closer to players than today, where more communication and interaction happens with agents and online approaches.

Winningham reminded me about the owner or General Manager taking contract agreements into their own hands. Marge Schott was the owner of the Cincinnati Reds, actually titled as President and CEO. She had her own idea of a gadget to manage players and player situations.

In 1989, she settled a salary dispute with outfielder Daniels by flipping a coin in the parking lot of the spring training complex on live TV. Daniel's agent, Lou Oppenheim, agreed to the "gadget." Schott called heads. Her half-dollar coin came up tails. Daniels won the toss and turned $0.50 into an increase of an extra $25,000.

Players never really know, nor can they plan their interactions with Owners and General Managers.

Chapter 20: Dan Evans — A True Baseball Authority

When researching anything related to managing the show, it's best to make sure that anyone with baseball management is talked to if available.

When talking to Dan Evans, you quickly learn that he has been there and done that. Not only that, he is still involved in the game in different ways. Dan Evan's twitter profile states that he is a former General Manager of the Los Angeles Dodgers and a baseball authority. His resume and accomplishments certainly add up to his authority status. Quite simply, he has been described as a good baseball mind and a solid evaluator of talent. His experience is clearly unique and wide-ranging.

Dan will tell you that he is, first and foremost, a baseball fan.

As well as being the former General Manager of the Los Angeles Dodgers, Dan has been in decision-making roles in professional baseball for nearly four decades, holding decision-making positions with five major league franchises. His baseball career includes stints with the Chicago White Sox, Chicago Cubs, Los Angeles Dodgers, Seattle Mariners, and as

Director of Pacific Rim Operations for the Toronto Blue Jays. He also acts as a consultant for numerous sports and worldwide baseball-related matters.

Today, he runs a baseball consulting company, from which he provides experienced advice in decision-making, staff, procedures, strategy, and resources of baseball organizations.

Besides being widely known for his expertise and success in the MLB, he was one of the pioneers to use technology & video analysis.

Dan Evans was GM of the Dodgers and White Sox, famously bringing in players like Michael Jordan and Bo Jackson and hiring former Marlins GM Kim Ng (she just recently announced her stepping down from her Marlins GM position).

Dan Evans began his career with the White Sox as an intern. He is a Chicago guy. He eventually became the Assistant General Manager for the White Sox. During his time with the team, he helped them land stars like Frank Thomas, Paul Konerko, Robin Ventura, and Jack McDowell, amongst others. Obviously, the list of players he helped bring in is loaded with significant game-changing abilities for his organizations. By significant, I mean wins, and that's the goal of any General Manager.

In talking with Dan, many intrinsic qualities come to light:

- He credits his many mentors in his career and always talks about his great parents. He says that he learned from some great people. He has tried to impart some of that to the organizations he has worked and consulted for.

- His early interest in baseball resulted from attending a three-week-long baseball camp. To this day, he talks about this sports camp that changed his life. Not only did he gain tremendous baseball skills, but, as he tells it, it gave him confidence and made him a far more experienced and mature person.

- In 2000, Dan walked away from an incredible baseball job with the White Sox without his next job lined up. He stated that he just needed a new challenge. He adds that he was thrilled to take that risk.

- Because of important people in his life who passed away, he decided, and will state it, that he was going to enjoy the heck out of life every step of the way. That means just being Dan Evans. Part of that means not being afraid to take chances and explore. That philosophy, he feels, as a former General Manager or not, has elevated his own being.

- People don't leave when they're in a great environment, and it doesn't have to be a championship or a flashy environment: just a positive workplace, a place where values, equality, and equity are all in place.
- Dan always promotes the fact that you have to dream big.
- Don't be afraid of change because with change comes a different outlook, viewpoints, influencers, mentors, and a different work environment you've never been in.

Dan was heard in one of his many interviews that he continues to learn, enjoy, and explore.

These qualities and more made him, at the time, the epitome of a baseball General Manager and led to his many successes in baseball and in life.

Dan can talk about baseball, facts, statistics, metrics, trades, philosophies, and much more, but one thing he is loud and clear about is his interaction, relationships, and working with the people. Every General Manager speaks of the people component as a major element and its importance in their job. A lot of that, for Dan, is from learning from great people along his career path.

When asking Dan about his favorite part of a General Manager's job and working in sports in general, he speaks of the personal relationships he has gained all over the world.

Dan is big on communication. All General Managers have to be. Evans states that people at the top have to be communicative leaders. Thinking from his own experiences, they have to be people who don't approach things as someone working for them but more of working with them.

Good leaders take ideas from every element and every avenue of input. Even an intern can be invited to contribute. Dan Evans was that intern at one point.

Stifling creativity stifles communication. Too much stifling leads to people looking for opportunities to leave. People don't leave when they're in a great environment. That environment doesn't necessarily have to be a championship environment: just a positive workplace, a place where values, equality, food, communication, and equity are all in place. In this same breath, he states that it doesn't hurt to dream big.

Great leaders are great communicators. Through their communication skills, they show and demonstrate their true vision. Their vision permeates through the rest of the organization positively. Dan

Evans will tell you that is something he has tried to instill in every group he has been in.

Baseball requires a lot of personal interaction and interpersonal relationships due to the length of the days and its season, along with the game's worldwide popularity. As a result, developing numerous long-standing relationships is key. That's what he treasures while working in the sport of baseball.

It is a huge sport, but the people who work in the game are still close-knit and are usually a phone call away.

Dan Evans states, "Getting to know people that you either compete with on a daily basis or associate with due to their involvement in the game makes the entire work experience even better."

Many General Managers having hectic days can take note here.

Dan has talked freely about the staff he developed with the GM of the Dodgers. He and his staff accomplished a turnaround of the franchise, rapidly transforming and restoring the organization into a player development and scouting-oriented club that they had once been in other successful years. Again, the people-orientation and emphasis as the organization's leader continues to bubble to the top of Dan's approach and success.

We started out by stating that Dan Evans is a baseball authority. After this, you can see his authority extends way beyond the sport.

Chapter 21: Dick Williams Laid the Foundation for Today's Successes

Sometimes, looking at a non-conventional approach to general management can create new ideas and inspiration for future organizations. That is the case with Dick Williams. The product of a multi-generational connection to Reds ownership, Dick Williams, with his grandfather, father and uncle maintaining ownership of the Cincinnati Reds at some point to now, is the club's former President of baseball operations/GM.

With a business of a non-baseball background, Williams brought with him a new set of baseball ideas. His ideas helped bring the Cincinnati Reds closer to what many called modern baseball while catching up to other teams around the league.

As reported by Steve Mancuso, writer of the Reds Content Plus blog, "Dick Williams took the lead on modernizing every aspect of baseball operations. Dick was the mastermind behind building the spring training facility in Goodyear, AZ, drove advances in the Red's scouting and player development systems, expanded the team's capacity for analytics, and established the Red's sports science departments."

Under Dick, Mancuso talks about how the Reds strengthened their farm system by growing their amateur scouting and player development staffs, implemented analytics initiatives that included the additions of both personnel and infrastructure, strengthened the scouting presence in the Pacific Rim and Latin America, and became one of the first teams in baseball to establish a sports science and wellness department.

Williams also rebuilt scouting stations in the Dominican Republic, Venezuela, Panama, Colombia, Mexico, and Nicaragua. Current Red's President of baseball operations, Nick Krall, plainly stated, "We changed a lot of different things about what we do."

The essence of Williams' changes and way of management were categorized as the transformation of an organization from a rusty, out-of-date operation into the game's most modern one.

Williams' changes and ways came from a creative mind and weren't necessarily on this General Manager's to-do list at the beginning.

Much of this change took time to get traction. Many of the organization's successes and even wins in the current and next seasons are due to the fruit-bearing efforts of Dick Williams.

Other General Manager or, in Williams' case, President of baseball operations changes included moving from three coaches to four for each baseball affiliate. This was clearly, at the time, a new investment in minor-league player development.

Another Williams-attributed change was expanding the use of technology within the organization. In 2019, it was said that the "data revolution" had arrived for the Red's pitching staff and coaches. Williams brought the previous outsourced technology to the spring training facility in Goodyear. If you want specifics, by 2020, every spring training mound had Rapsodo, Edgertronic, and an intern with an iPad behind the mound to relay real-time info about each pitch.

Sure, players talk about their teams and the changes that are going on. When you hear positive comments, that usually is an indication of success now or certainly in the future.

Tejay Antone, Cincinnati Reds reliever, was drafted by the Reds in 2014. He saw the old regime and the new regime under Williams. In February 2021, Antone made his thoughts public about the impact of the changes that Dick Williams was responsible for.

Antone wrote: "Wow, what a difference it is today. I can't thank our front office enough for investing in the development side and being at the forefront of not only technology but having the right people in place to relay and educate us players about what the technology is saying. A lot of players are begging to be with the Reds because of our player development. I'm not sure I would have made it to the big leagues if it wasn't for people like Eric Jagers, Kyle Boddy, and many others."

It was said in the chapter title, laying the foundation for today's successes. Looking back at what Williams did, one can clearly see his mark on the Reds' current roster.

Dick Williams, in his general management style or then President of baseball operations, looked at every inch and corner of the organization. His views were from the perspective of his business past. His business background gave him insight into the value of things like delegation and data-driven decisions.

As President of baseball operations, Dick Williams was working for an owner or, in the Red's case, an ownership group. Typically, the types of changes he made can run up against ownership pushback, right or wrong. Williams had the clout with that ownership group to make the changes he wanted, even though some of those changes were significant, gambles, and unconventional.

That makes for a successful General Manager and/or President of baseball operations. Dick Williams laid that foundation.

Dick Williams has been gone from the Reds since 2020, pursuing non-baseball interests and more family time.

Chapter 22: Ben Cherington — From Player Development to Team Development

Ben Cherington has been the General Manager of the Pittsburgh Pirates since November 2019. During his time as GM of the Pirates, Cherington made plenty of trades and roster moves and did all the things a General Manager does and should do to revamp the team in Pittsburgh.

Ben Cherington entered the 2023 season as the relatively new General Manager with a situation that had to be changed. After a couple of seasons with over 100 losses, it was like the team had taken two steps backward.

It was time for a step forward. Cherington got the green light from his ownership to spend $30 million in free agency in the offseason, signing six veterans to supplement the young core of players and prospects, allowing the Pirates to start the season in much better shape with much different results (positive). That's what General Managers do or should do.

"Although it goes without saying," Cherington said, "It's time to start getting better. It's a different time in our evolution."

General managers always have 'improving the team' on their to-do list.

Ben Cherington is deemed as one of the youngest 'veterans' in the game of baseball. He has already worked his way through every aspect of baseball operations and, over the years, has gained a well-rounded set of experiences at a high level that will help him guide this franchise to its next World Championship.

Cherington was the Boston GM, then served as Boston's Senior Vice President and Assistant General Manager since January 2009. In that role, he worked closely with Theo Epstein on all Major League personnel matters, including evaluation and analysis, player acquisition, and contract negotiation.

While we did expect Cherington's answer to the question of what a typical day is to be the same or similar to other General Managers' answers, he did lead with something a little different.

He categorized his days and work during the year according to the time of the year. He mentioned that November is much different than March, and March is different than July. Translated, this is the time right after the postseason ends and is different from pre-season and spring training, while pre-season is different from the month or time before the MLB trade deadline. You can just about divide up the duties by using this scheduling template.

The common thread is that every day brings the opportunity to try to solve problems and find ways for the team to perform better on the field. That part of his answer to a typical day or workflow is consistent with most, if not all General Managers.

It would be surprising not to hear a GM talk about improving their team and performing better on the field. The General Manager's attitude, mindset, and approach always have to be consistent and of a winning nature.

When asked by a reporter late in the season, Cherington stated, "We talk about getting better all the time; I've got to get better. We all have to get better. We all want to win. We all have our jobs to make that happen. And I believe our field manager is doing everything he can do to put us in the best position to compete and win."

Ben has stated that he and his staff are privileged to work in baseball.

During the off-season, if there is an off-season, Cherington states that it's still very busy. Instead of supporting and watching the team actively playing games, the focus shifts to the strategies and decisions, hoping to make the team strong for the future. This includes player acquisition, staffing decisions, and a whole lot more.

Right after the post-season is a time to develop and refine plans that eventually are executed, especially from November to January. Every team works this way, and it creates an even more competitive environment, which is the fun part, according to Ben.

While the work changes depending on the season, Ben Cherington states that regardless of the season, his favorite part of the job is working with a tremendously talented group of people trying to work towards that same goal of getting better and winning more games. That favorite part is contrasted with his least favorite part, which is the personal sacrifice related to spending time with family. He truly misses that through the year, much less the season.

With that time spent on the job, we asked him what he does during each game. His response was quick. He watches every pitch. Other General Managers treat games differently, but Ben was right to the point. While he allocates time to watch his team, it makes it difficult for him to watch other games to track competition and check out other players. When not watching his team play, he spends a lot of time in meetings, on the phone, interviewing people, managing operational issues, managing the budget, and performing other duties, much like any other leadership role.

In all of the conversations with various General Managers, scouting always comes up as a key component to building a team and eventual success. When you have a General Manager like Ben Cherington with a background in scouting, you have a greater probability of picking the right players, building the right roster, and succeeding.

Cherington has scouting in his background, much like many other General Managers who have climbed the ladder. He began his professional baseball career with the Cleveland Indians as an advanced scout in 1998. Continuing his scouting path, he joined the Red Sox organization in 1999 as a Mid-Atlantic area scout before becoming a baseball operations assistant that May.

Cherington continued through other positions with Boston, including Coordinator of International Scouting, Assistant Director of Player Development, and Director of Player Development. Cherington understands scouting. Cherington understands player development and that all bodes well when acquiring players and building rosters.

One of the ways to acquire players and build rosters is in-season and free agent trading. Almost all of these trades are done between Ben's General Manager counterparts involved in baseball operations. Sometimes, it's General Manager to General Manager, and sometimes, he depends on conversations between his Assistant General Managers and Assistant General Managers of other teams. Other conversations also happen. There are many, what he describes as stakeholders, involved in the communication, and it is all important to their goals, regardless of the season they are in.

For his team, the manager has very important input into trades. In his current situation, he has a field manager who is very baseball-smart and really knows all angles of the game. He never gave this a second thought. It's a valuable asset in his work. It's interesting to see the balance he works within. He understands that his field manager has input on roster decisions, with Ben, as the General Manager, having the final call. On the other hand, Ben has great input on the deployment of players in games, but his field manager has the final call on that.

Trading in the ranks of major league baseball is always a personal thing. It's always interesting to learn how each General Manager approaches trades. With the Pittsburgh Pirates, Ben Cherington is the one who tells a player that he has been traded, cut, or sent down to the next lower league. Ben thinks it's important that players hear directly from him whenever any kind of transaction, usually a trade, is made.

Cherington has mentioned before that he knows that sometimes luck is involved during the season. He still focuses on doing the things that will improve the team. He terms it positive productivity and incremental improvement. Not only does he consult his field manager on trades, but he also gives him full credit for keeping the team's focus on playing with the fullest effort, win or loss, no matter the results. Current field manager Derek Shelton accepts the accolades and responsibility from Cherington as he prides himself on his team always playing hard.

With Ben's background in player development, I asked him what his interaction is like with his player development managers. He spends time with them as his to-do list allows but would like to spend more time with them. He really likes his interaction with minor league managers. He is proud of the people leading his minor league teams. They, like him, put their heart and soul into helping young players develop, improve and mature. Spending time in this area is one of the true joys of his general management job.

Cherington is a former member of the advisory board for Good Sports, a Boston-based non-profit that distributes sports equipment to community organizations offering programs to disadvantaged youth, and has run the Boston Marathon and the New York Marathon in support of the charity. He has also participated in the Pan-Mass Challenge, which benefits the Dana-Farber Cancer Institute, and the 9K Run to Home Base, which raises funds for the Red Sox Foundation and Massachusetts General Hospital Home Base Program. It's nice to see he has a life outside the 24/7 demands of being a baseball General Manager.

Chapter 23: The Draft – Selecting the Future

Most sports fans have heard of the respective drafts for various sports. Baseball is one of those sports that has an active draft. Simply stated, the Major League Baseball draft is the primary method for assigning amateur baseball players from high schools, colleges, and others to its teams.

The first round of MLB's first-year player draft represents the potential to get the best players available in the United States (There are different rules, times, and procedures for international drafting). Being drafted is one thing. Making it to the big leagues is another. Approximately 66 percent of first-round picks end up playing in the major leagues.

As mentioned, most sports have a draft. Baseball has different draft characteristics compared to other sports. For instance, in the NFL, most players selected early in an NFL draft will start or see significant playing time the very next season, especially first-round draftees. That is not the case in baseball, as players go through a more methodical development process leading to the big leagues.

While we have the draft, the role of the general manager and the importance he places on the draft is key here.

Baseball officials for all 30 MLB teams enter into their busiest time of the season starting in July. The MLB Draft is three weeks into the month. The August 1st trade deadline is after that, and in between, usually around July 25th, teams must sign drafted players.

The General Manager's role in the first-year player draft in baseball is much different than in other sports. For some teams, the actual role of the GM in the MLB draft may be limited. For others, their role is more active. Typically, the person most important in the draft is the scouting director or the managers of the various scouting departments if there is more than one.

When you watch the draft, he is usually the one submitting the pick. Most of the time, he is the one phoning and informing the drafted player, but the GM, and sometimes the owner, also get involved with this. Now, with the scouting director's draft pick, the General Manager, team President, and owner are maintaining veto power. The credit for a successful draft goes to the scouting director.

How important is the draft? Some General Managers use the draft as the base foundation for all player and team development, rebuilding, and even future trade strategies.

Bill Dewitt, Owner and General Manager in 1965, drafted Hall of Fame catcher Johnny Bench in the second round that year. They also drafted and got high school third baseman Bernie Carbo with their first selection, who was a big part of the 1970 World Series team before getting traded in 1972. Hal McRae was also drafted that same year in the sixth round. Most know Hal as a Kansas City Royal player, but he contributed to the Big Red Machine in the early '70s. That's how important a draft can be to a team.

After the draft, the process begins, and the time comes for the General Manager to get contracts completed with as many players as possible and to get their pro careers started. This begins at the team's developmental facilities, mostly the same as spring training facilities, and then, hopefully for the more successful players, the Minor Leagues.

Different teams have different approaches to the MLB draft each year depending on their needs, gaps, trade strategies, etc. As an example, Kiley McDaniel of ESPN recently wrote about one team in particular.

He stated, "They draft position players and have settled on a pretty specific type. Power must be present, along with at least decent bat-to-ball skills, ideally with some physical skills and/or speed/defensive value."

This is a General Manager's approach and a particular strategy for a particular draft.

Other strategies revolve around drafting particular position players, the best player available at the time, the age of players, high school or college players, and more.

Other General Manager draft strategies are things like:

1. Drafting shortstops. Shortstops are often the quicker and most athletic players. Some teams draft shortstops, hoping to shift them to 2nd base or other positions.

2. Drafting catchers. The catcher position is a tough, grueling position. If a team is in need of a future backup here, they draft a catcher. Many catchers have shifted to play first base and designated hitter.

3. Draft pitchers. Most will talk of control pitchers. Wikipedia and other baseball General Managers define control pitchers as finesse pitchers who succeed mostly by using accurate pitches, as opposed to power pitchers. It's often said that good pitching beats good hitting, and you can never have too much pitching. Looking back at baseball history, filling a roster with and drafting high-profile pitchers has been a key to many successful teams. The early George Steinbrenner Yankee teams come to mind.

Ben Cherington, General Manager of the Pittsburgh Pirates, told Pittsburgh Baseball after the 2022 Major League draft, "We were looking for the best players. I think once you get to a certain part of the draft, you start looking at where we can impact the system in the best way. We have to be mindful of areas in the system where we've already got a lot of players, but we didn't go into the draft looking to add a certain number of pitchers."

That gives you an idea of how a General Manager thinks and approaches the draft.

Although, not a General Manager, Orioles Director of Draft Operations Brad Ciolek said to put your best foot forward, do your homework, do your due diligence on all fronts, and do your best to take the player. Ultimately, it's up to them and how quickly they ascend in the system and major league baseball.

Honestly, trade strategies are all over the place with many variations, plus they change every year depending on where a club sits with their strategy, performance, and success and what new gaps they have.

Bill Schmidt, General Manager of the Colorado Rockies, was quite involved and oversaw the draft for the Rockies for many years. With his scouting background and now his general management role, he immersed himself in the draft each year. Every draft year is different. It's more than numbers. Asking Bill what he looks for in a player before drafting is more than the obvious.

With Schmidt being a people person and really liking the people part of his job, he dives deep into the person more than batting averages and ERAs. He likes to find out what really makes them go, what their motivations are and what values do they have. This goes so far as understanding how each individual was born and raised.

He follows their path from beginning to end. All of this allows him to get to know players as a total person. Schmidt probes into things like managing money, how they handle adversity, and all that could translate into managing a season. He now stresses that mental makeup is most important. Sure, they look at the baseball fundamentals, but his experience says that he's good at finding fundamentals but works hard not to miss any aspects of a person's makeup. He really wants to understand the things that cause someone to behave a certain way, their feelings, opinions, concerns, likes, dislikes, etc. That's the basis of someone's true personality and is important when evaluating and ranking players ahead of the draft.

Schmidt states that in a draft, you don't know what's going to happen. There is a little bit of luck involved. Luck can't rule, so you have to be prepared for any curveballs or opportunities that might come your way. That's the draft.

While it's different for all teams, a lot of credit for successful drafts goes mostly to strong scouting directors with special evaluative skills. They are supported by many others. These employees work very hard, are underrated, and are probably underpaid. These consist of Assistant General Managers, people in analytics, scouts, and minor league managers.

Different General Managers (past and present) approach the draft differently.

In previous drafts and when he was a General Manager, Theo Epstein had input on the first couple of rounds. He was careful not to overrule picks that scouts felt strongly about. Epstein participated in draft preparation meetings, a point of the process where he used his General Manager's influence. His opinion was that the draft belonged to the scouting director.

However, a good team, like the Red Sox, often reached a consensus under his management. Epstein was fine with this process and the ensuing results. He rarely vetoed his scouting director's picks.

Doug Melvin, the previous General Manager and now Senior adviser to the Milwaukee Brewers, only viewed players at pre-draft workouts, usually on their home field. The scouting director makes the final decision for the Brewers, but Melvin has input on a few players when it comes to the character of a potential draft pick.

John Mozeliak of the St. Louis Cardinals also has the scouting director make all of the draft selections for the team.

Kevin Towers, who served as the Arizona Diamondbacks' General Manager from 2010 to 2014, had their draft picks determined by their scouting director and his Vice President of scouting and player development. Both received Towers' opinion if needed but made the decision on picks. Both are held accountable for the draft. Since this is the case, Towers stays out of it unless asked.

The scouting director made the decisions in all the draft rounds. At the time, the club's philosophy was to take and carry players with the highest potential or the highest probability of reaching those potentials.

Braves' former Frank Wren: he has always believed to have a valid opinion in the draft room, you have to immerse yourself in it full-time. He won't make any selections for the club, but he is involved in the draft and will give opinions based on the team's scouting reports.

Alex Anthopoulos is the General Manager of the Atlanta Braves. Previously, he was the General Manager of the Toronto Blue Jays. Since his reign started in 2009, they were known for having consistently strong drafts, which built a strong farm system known as one of the best in the game at that time.

His risk level was higher than average as he drafted a large number of high school players, both pitchers and position players. His eye for young talent was considered extraordinary. Many of his top draft picks gave a performance greater than expected during their development.

In a more current setting, Astros' General Manager Dana Brown spent much time with the team's scouts reviewing information on numerous players.

Brown said, "This is probably the fun part of the job because it's something that I'm so used to. We're going through all these names, and we're having conversations, and I'm bringing a lot of my philosophies and my thought processes to it, and so it's actually exciting, and it's refreshing to be able to talk about some upcoming young players."

Brown was hired primarily because of his ability to spot talented prospects. The Astros were in great need of new talent in their farm system that had ranked close to the bottom of the rankings. This was primarily due to a lack of success in the early draft rounds.

Brown also stated, "It's all about nailing the draft; the draft is the future of the organization, and at the end of the day, you have to take good players. There's just no excuse."

Chapter 24: Free Agency – Part of the Roster Building Puzzle

Jason Heyward, you've heard of him, was one of the few who made his major league debut (on Opening Day in 2010) and never returned to the Minor Leagues. By the time the 2015 season ended, Heyward had clocked in six years of service. At that point, according to MLB rules, he became eligible for free agency. Heyward took advantage of that and signed an eight-year contract with the Cubs. That's exactly the kind of deal you see or General Managers want and like as they use free agency to build their rosters.

MLB free agency is perhaps the most important and significant change of hands, rearranging and reordering during an MLB year. This then places a substantial emphasis on making prudent, sensible, and intelligent free agent signings that help a team sometimes in the short term but mostly in the long run, as General Managers think and plan.

While most reading this will know what a free agent in major league baseball is, it may be worth restating the concept here for others.

While we won't go into the nitty-gritty details of the history of the MLB free agency, we will state that Free agency in MLB has existed since the 1972 Flood vs. Kuhn Supreme Court case, well known around baseball. One of the landmark decisions that came from that case was a decision that destroyed what was known as the "reserve clause" in baseball.

From this came the signing of a new agreement. That agreement, signed at the All-Star break in 1976, stated that any player with six years of Major League experience could become a free agent.

As you can tell by its name, free agency means that players are free to sign with whichever team they please. Under free agency, players are free to negotiate with the teams interested in their services and sign agreed-upon contracts. Usually, those contracts follow the market value of a player.

In the free agency market, General Managers can choose to sign whoever they want to try and upgrade certain positions in their current lineup to put together a winning team. The question comes down to how much a team is willing to pay for a player's services or if another team is willing to pay more. It's funny that some of the older generation General Managers called this an "auction" and chose not to participate in the bidding and buying.

Officially, players become free agents the day after the conclusion of the World Series. However, their signing period doesn't start until five days after the conclusion of the World Series.

The period for signing Major League Baseball's free agents lasts for several months. Starting on November 3rd at 9:00 am ET in 2021, all players on expiring contracts are officially free agents. They can start meeting with teams right away but will have to wait at least five days before being able to sign with other clubs.

One of the decisions teams have to make is with regard to their contract options for players entering "team-option" years.

As we mentioned, free agents can sign with teams at any point through the offseason. This can even drift over to the beginning of the following season. Needless to say, most major transactions happen during the first couple of weeks or the first month or two of free agency. Last-minute signings are mostly reserved for injured players or more veteran players.

As soon as an MLB season ends, all players who have expiring contracts become free agents. They have to respect that five-day rule before officially signing with another club. The whole basis is that free agency allows athletes at the peak of their careers to shop themselves out to teams willing to pay top dollar and offer the most comprehensive benefits and perks.

John Schuerholz spent 26 seasons as a big-league GM with the Royals but mostly the Braves, winning 16 division titles, six pennants, and two World Series Championships.

Schuerholz showed expertise in how to retool his team. He had a sense of which holes could be filled by integrating prospects and those that needed outside solutions.

Schuerholz also was not typically a participant in the big-name free agent signings. He actually referred to the free agent market for player auctions.

General managers in the free agency market look for players and choose who they sign. General Managers look at the available players on the free agent market and compare them to their team's current roster to evaluate whether an increase in productivity can be gained by signing a free agent player working towards putting together a winning team. As John Schuerholz described, it is competitive and can turn into an auction.

One thing to note, to help prevent any gamesmanship from owners, agents, and players, is that free agent signings come with a 3-month trade restriction from the day of signing.

How did MLB work before free agency? The only negotiating leverage of most players was to hold out at contract time and to refuse to play unless their conditions were met. Players were bound to negotiate a new contract to play another year for the same team or to ask to be released or traded.

Today, the league's free agent carousel is sometimes a very hopeful time of the year. General Managers add new players to their teams who they hope will push them to the next level of becoming championship contenders. Sometimes, that is a viable strategy for a General Manager, and sometimes, that strategy backfires.

According to MLB.com, Tony Sipp was released by the Padres in May 2014, after he had between four and five years of Major League service time. Sipp subsequently signed a guaranteed Major League contract with the Astros that ran through the end of the 2014 season. Sipp was eligible for salary arbitration, not free agency, because he finished the season with less than six years of Major League service time. Sipp qualified as a free agent following the next season (2015) and re-signed with the Astros on a three-year deal.

Nick Krall of the Cincinnati Reds has stated, "If there is a contract that makes sense for us, we will pursue it."

This was after Krall signed two free agents at the time, Will Myers and Curt Casali, to one-year deals.

"We've talked about this over the last few years. We have to be a team that builds from within, but at the same time, we have to bring solid players around our young players. It's one person at a time, one decision at a time, and that's how we're going to evaluate any contract decision."

This applies to free agent signings for the Reds and is a common and appropriate approach for many General Managers.

Sometimes, free agent signings are very successful. The New York Yankees signed Reggie Jackson to a five-year, $2.9 million contract. That amount is nothing nowadays, but it was huge in the 1970s.

Reggie Jackson proved his worth for every penny of that contract once signed. The former Baltimore Orioles and Oakland Athletics hitter was an all-star every season of the deal. During that time, he was part of a team that won two World Series titles. Just one monumental statistic was that he hit 12 home runs in 34 playoff games during his time with the Yankees. That made the Yankees big fans of free agent signings, and we've seen them spend freely since.

Some free agents are flops.

The Seattle Mariners had a few dismal seasons in a row leading up to the 2004 season. In fact, they had the worst offense at the time. They were bound and determined to fix that problem and turned to the free agency market. Through their scouting and research, they landed on Adrian Beltre.

Beltre had been with the Dodgers and was considered to be an average hitter during his first six seasons. After that, in 2004, his performance exploded. He hit 48 home runs and had an OPS over 1,000. That caught the eye of the Mariners as a potential plug for their gap(s).

They awarded Beltre a large five-year contract and made him the key piece of their lineup. Sorry to say that Beltre didn't put up those big numbers again and went back to the average classification. It was reported that he never hit for a .300 average and didn't get close to a 30-home run season. He did go on to a stellar career elsewhere, but Seattle didn't have a good free agent with that player at that time.

Andy MacPhail was General Manager of the Minnesota Twins from 1985 to 1994. He had much success quickly upon taking the reins of the team. The Minnesota team was considered a lower-revenue, small to medium-sized market team. Despite his quick success, MacPhail recognized that he needed a solid crop of low-salaried players, rookies or other prospects, and even under-appreciated veterans who had been around and could ripen further. This low-salaried approach was made available to fill his gaps with free agents.

When he was General Manager in Chicago, he used a similar approach. He did emphasize player development to build a team but, at the same time, still wanted to bring veteran players in to help keep his team competitive in what he called, at the time, a weak division. The way to accomplish this was with free agent signings since free agency was in play at that time.

Not everyone who was a baseball General Manager jumped into the free agent foray. Jim Campbell was General Manager and was involved in many high levels for a long time with the Detroit Tigers from 1949-1992. His team hit a period of struggles. Despite the team's struggles, Campbell spurned the opportunities presented by the introduction of free agency in 1976.

For many years, he signed no free agent. Instead, he relied on great success from his scouting department in areas of draft or trades. Through the latter part of his tenure with Detroit, he continued to de-emphasize free agency. He resorted to his old ways when it came to sourcing talent. He built champion-level teams without relying on free agents.

He eventually succumbed to free agent signings. He was successful with the Atlanta Braves in the 1990's. That success dwindled after a successful run because the farm system could not continue producing stars like it had. This final put pressure on Schuerholz's trades and led to more free agent signings.

SOURCING: Some of the facts and details above are used with permission from Mark Armour, Author of "In Pursuit of Pennants – Baseball Operations from Deadball to Moneyball."

Chapter 25: The Globalization of Baseball and International Players

Although baseball remains America's pastime, the game has expanded beyond America and has become an important sport across the globe. Maybe it's time to call baseball the World's Pastime.

While much has been written about international baseball markets, the emphasis here is a focus on what General Managers must manage.

Today, every MLB team is involved in international signings.

Look at any organization chart for any MLB team, and you will see position after position with descriptive titles. In looking at these, those involved with international work stand out. This is just a small sampling of teams:

- Cincinnati Reds — Senior Director, International Scouting, Asst. Dir., Player Dev. & Int'l Scouting, International Scouting Analyst, Director, South America Scouting, Director, Caribbean Scouting.

- Boston Red Sox — Co-Directors, International Scouting, Manager, International Scouting.

- Chicago Cubs — Vice President, International Scouting, Senior Director, International Player Development and Operations, Assistant, International Scouting.

- Tampa Bay Rays — Director, International Scouting, Coordinator, International Scouting.

- Los Angeles Dodgers — Vice President, International Scouting, Assistant Director, International Scouting, Manager, International Scouting

Teams have realized that teams that invest abroad stand to reap a competitive advantage in the years to come; thus, it is a well-structured international effort.

It's no wonder you see a situation where the 2023 Opening Day rosters featured one of MLB's most internationally diverse players. A total of 268 internationally-born players representing 19 countries or territories outside the United States were on 2023's Opening Day rosters. This added up to

28.5 percent of the total number of players on Opening Day rosters.

Major League Baseball is focused on increasing awareness of baseball beyond the U.S. across the globe. They now have offices throughout Asia, Europe, and Latin America. There is much work to target new fans, existing fans, and players, all with the ultimate goal of making baseball a global passion. With this awareness comes more player availability and more players eager to play in the MLB.

"Countries outside of the United States remain an important source of Major League players, and we want to do all we can to promote the health of the game in those countries," said Morgan Sword, who oversees all international signings as part of his duties as Senior Vice President of league economics and operations for Major League Baseball.

"We hope to improve our system of player acquisition and create a better working relationship with the trainer community of Latin America."

The dramatic increase in Latin players in the major leagues is due to several factors. First, the major league expansion that began in 1961 when the major leagues increased to 30 teams, owners were forced to look for more avenues of player acquisition.

The Dominican Republic has what is known as a rich baseball culture. They truly do have an abundance of baseball talent, starting with the country's emphasis on developing young players.

The international talent market is loaded with players just waiting to be discovered. Venezuela and the Dominican Republic have shown to have a lot of talent, as well as emerging player markets in China, Brazil, Europe, and Colombia.

Given all this, a General Manager has to manage those involved in international scouting and operations as another component of player acquisition.

When signing international prospects, the goal is to have these players succeed in the club's Minor League system and eventually play in the big leagues. It's also a strategy to package young international talent in trades in exchange for missing pieces to fill the roster and player development gaps. That is one reason you find many General Managers active on the international front.

International scouting continues to evolve on an ongoing basis. Data, technology, information, and more funding have allowed amateur baseball to show continued growth across borders. With this growth comes scouting. With more growth comes more scouting.

Many General Managers have come up through the scouting ranks. Many of them have dabbled in international scouting. Now, they have to elevate that and manage anything international. There are drafts, player development, and MLB rules involved that they or someone on their staff gets involved with.

Regarding international scouting, most would say that Latin America is the most important. The number of international scouts varies from team to team, but every organization has a significant presence when scouting the Latin American countries.

Most clubs have area scouts in both Venezuela and the Dominican Republic. When looking at most of these organizations, you will see five scouts working in the Dominican Republic. On average, Venezuela typically will have four scouts; however, many Venezuelan players go to Columbia for exposure. These international scouts are responsible for all of the talent and prospects in their region of particular countries.

Many teams have a full-time evaluator/scout in Mexico. In countries like Mexico, the scout will work on both the professional and amateur levels. Some teams extend this and have full-time scouts in Curaçao, Nicaragua, Panama, or the Bahamas as well.

With this globalization, you can now see that every major league team has a hierarchy of international workers.

While baseball is highly American, it attracts and employs a diverse set of multi-lingual fans, players, coaches, and managers. Because of this, teams employ translation and interpretation as the diversity increases.

Because Major League Baseball relies on talent from all over the world, translation and interpretation become a requirement.

Since 2016, teams have been required to have at least two full-time Spanish language interpreters. MLB started requiring all 30 teams to hire at least one full-time, year-round translator for its Spanish-speaking baseball players. This directive was an effort to provide Spanish-speaking players with language assistance when it came to communication with the coaching staff, teammates, and reporters during press conferences and interviews.

The percentage of Spanish-speaking players in major league baseball is currently about 28%. In the minor league, those numbers increase to 41%.

Things are a bit different for Asian players. Typically, you will find Asian players working with their personal interpreters. There is not enough of a presence yet to warrant MLB requiring teams to have full-time interpreters for these players, but the league is working on this.

Many teams have a foreign language interpreter listed on their organization chart. In the case of the Toronto Blue Jays, they call that person a Bilingual Player Interpreter.

General Managers know that international players are developed much earlier than in the U.S. General managers tend to combine international player development with international scouting.

Patience pays off. Signing young international players, along with patience, can result in a better-than-average payoff for any team.

Chapter 26: Winter and General Manager Meetings – Where Things Happen

Fred Claire, formerly of the Dodgers, started his general management work knowing his team's gaps and went to work to address them. The first place he turned to was the one attended by every General Manager. That place is the General Manager's winter meetings, always a place for active discussion, trades, and other conversations.

Every General Manager looks forward to these meetings, and because of that, it is worth a quick review of those meetings from the perspective of a General Manager.

Throughout our conversations with various General Managers, we have tried to figure out the seasons: pre-season, regular season, post-season, and off-season. The bottom line is there are not as definitive lines between the seasons as these labels indicate.

We know that the regular season kicks off right at the end of March or the very beginning of April.

Regardless of these labels, the business of baseball never stops.

There is lots of activity, in part during the season and mostly in the labeled offseason. This activity includes signing free agents, trades, drafts, and getting ready for spring training. Some of this activity can happen and be further planned when executives and representatives from all 30 teams gather in the same room. Where does it happen? MLB's Winter Meetings.

Winter meetings are considered one of the more important events of the baseball year. It is an opportunity for league executives, major and minor league representatives, owners, and other higher-up baseball people to convene to discuss league business. Trades happen during these meetings, and the Rule 5 draft happens here.

From the MLB website, the Winter Meetings are when "executives, team staff, media, exhibitors and job seekers converge to network with peers, fill job and internship vacancies, attend workshops, discuss trends and exchange ideas." These meetings are similar to trade shows, conferences, etc., for other jobs and professions, but for baseball.

The Winter Meetings date back to the 1876 season when William Hulbert was selected as baseball's first league president. Both New York Mutuals and Philadelphia Athletics were expelled for not playing all their assigned games. As they say in many instances of baseball, the rest is history. These meetings are now hosted in various cities, with many notable events, agreements, and deals taking place that impact the MLB.

NBC Sports reported that the 1975 Chicago White Sox went 75-86, finishing 22.5 games behind the Oakland A's in the AL West. They were a team in need of many things, but the best description is they needed a shakeup. White Sox owner at the time, Bill Veeck, who had just purchased the team literally days before, showed up at the Winter Meetings in Fort Lauderdale that year with a plan to make that shake-up happen.

Veeck sat down at a convenient table in the hotel lobby where the meetings were taking place and actually taped a sign to that table that read "Open for Business."

Veeck was known for his unconventional ways, stunts, humor, and doing things differently. By the time Veeck returned to his new Chicago office, he had negotiated six trades involving 22 players. He thanked MLB for having winter meetings.

Today, the meetings don't have Bill Veeck. The ones that now show up are more serious, geared for 24/7, 365-day business communicating via text and cell phones. The midnight mingling no longer takes place like Veeck participated in, which he later described as one of the things that makes baseball fun.

Those who attend the MLB Winter Meetings are either members of the National Association of Professional Baseball Leagues, Inc. (Minor League Baseball), Major League Baseball, or Approved Non-Members (every agent known to MLB and some that might not be as known), lawyers, accountants, visitors from baseball-playing countries, and accredited members of the press.

The meetings actually attract upwards of 3,000 people each year. In addition to member attendees, there are a range of league executives, team scouts, and other high-ranking principals.

With so many baseball people in one place, player trades and free agent signings are expected to happen, and they do. Aside from that activity, however, the informal meetings that used to take place in hotel lobbies up until the turn of the 20th century have been replaced by texting, cell phones, and emailing. The most pertinent interactions take place in the privacy of suites and private meeting rooms due to the multitude of media personnel and raving fans converging on the site.

Speaking of the fans, the winter meetings are described as the closest thing to Baseball Christmas a fan can get, whether a fan of a rebuilding or a team building a roster.

It's a time when teams set the stage for the upcoming season. Now that fans and the media know what is to happen, it is also a time filled with great anticipation and expectations like no other time of the season.

Here are some examples of the team's agenda going into the winter meetings:

- The Yankees went to look for a left fielder, monitoring the starting pitching market and aiming to improve the bullpen.

- The Blue Jays have three young, talented catchers whom half the league should be after. This is a rare opportunity for this organization, and while starting pitching and an outfielder remain top priorities, dealing with one of these catchers will also be in play.

- The O's want to add a starting pitcher who can slot into one of the top three spots in their rotation.

- The Rays need at least one quality left-handed bat to bolster their lineup.

- The Guardians need to start having critical conversations with other clubs to lay the groundwork for acquiring a catcher.

- The Royals are looking to acquire pitching this offseason, whether it's from the free agent or trade market.

- The Tigers need bats.

- The Mets badly need pitching. The Winter Meetings will give them a forum to address that need.

These examples are just a few that lead into the dynamics of the many conversations, deals, and announcements that take place at the winter meetings.

Just a quick note on General Manager Meetings:

The General Manager meetings are separate from the winter meetings. They are known to be a place where GMs and their staff spend more time discussing business about the game. The annual meeting of General Managers is the first big event of their offseason.

At the General Manager meeting, teams network and talk with fellow General Managers to begin laying the groundwork for potential trades that happen later in the offseason.

In addition to the networking, lobby conversations, conferences, and casual and formal meetings about league issues, the GM Meetings are usually used for teams to meet, talk about wants and needs, player values, and offseason plans and learn who plans to do what and who may be available as everyone looks to improve their position through the offseason.

In the past, November and the General Manager meetings were used mostly for research and analytical review. Actual deals and transactions then happened in early December at these winter meetings.

Picture this: a hotel lobby or ballroom filled with media types, all looking for stories and trading leads. Amongst these are team personnel and General Managers. Names are kicked around, "what-ifs" are discussed, proposals are swapped, and ideas are floated. Scenarios are planned and developed all with the future in mind. Every team wants to improve, and the General Managers are at the helm.

The winter meetings and the General Manager meetings are just more events added to the General Manager's calendar, all in addition to spring training, the regular season, and the post-season.

Managing the Show - Conclusion

The conclusion of Managing the Show is more of a summary and re-statement of the state of baseball, all with the wrapping up of anything and everything related to general management.

It all comes down to the point that Major League Baseball is in the business of producing, showcasing, and presenting human athletic (baseball) performance. The product of baseball consists of and always strives for more people to be the best at what they do.

That showcase is front and center for the millions who watch the sport for fun without having to play it. General Managers are fundamentally responsible for making and presenting the product and always try to make it better for their target market.

Baseball continues to make an imprint on America. There is much historical influence while representing culture to make this happen. It is, after all, a favorite sport. Add to this culture the economics of the game, the technological advances, and the human element and drama, and you can see how baseball supports and reflects many aspects of American Life.

Whatever you take from this book, you can easily see that being a baseball General Manager is not an easy job. It really is a job where one must still put up with the whims of an owner, whether they are active or not. The thinking that pervades every General Manager, and hopefully every owner, is "always try to make the team better."

In late 2023, the front-office chiefs for the Boston Red Sox and New York Mets were fired and not re-hired.

It was quoted, "It was a reminder of a reliable truth for ambitious baseball executives: Their fate is closely tied to their team owners' ambitions, and whether their bosses are more desperate to win or to save money. A General Manager has to report to those whims and ambitions."

What we have learned is that all general management jobs are different. They are a function of people, personalities, education, background, previous playing career, and more. There are aggressive and front-and-center showcasing General Managers, and there are more passive approaches by some General Managers. General Managers have a near-term and long-term focus. They have a short-

and long-term focus on player acquisition, player development, and player retention.

As it turns out, all of this activity and focus is broken down into seasons: pre-season, regular season, post-season, and off-season. If we were writing a how-to course, manual, or handbook for being a baseball General Manager, these would be the time period breakdowns.

A General Manager has a lot of different activities under his supervision. There is a growing importance of General Managers having an emphasis even more on long-term planning, analytics in all phases of the game and club operation, investments and prioritization in player development, domestically and internationally, drafting, scouting, and trades, not to mention everyday organizational challenges when people are involved.

In most organizations, the General Manager is in charge.

In talking with Nick Krall of the Cincinnati Reds and discussing the General Manager's title and position vs. the Director of baseball operations' title and job, he pointed out that those are just titles. There needs to be one person clearly in charge. He is that person in charge and reports to the owner of the club.

The owner relies on Nick to manage the club and make the necessary decisions.

After talking with Nick, it was clear that he lives by this principle and was in charge. With that comes a passion for his job. His team facilitates related decisions and approaches. One thing to note is that Nick Krall is clearly in charge and clearly a General Manager.

After the interview with Krall and his statements above about titles being titles and one person in charge, the Cincinnati Reds elevated, in late 2023, General Manager Nick Krall to the position of President of baseball operations, and Assistant GM Brad Meador had a title change and promotion to GM and Senior Vice-President.

The media reported, "While the hierarchy doesn't change — Krall remains the lead decision-maker and Meador, his top advisor — the changes reflect a front-office structure that's become more common throughout Major League Baseball in recent years."

"Nick has a great baseball mind and has shown exceptional leadership in advancing every aspect of our baseball operations," said Reds owner Bob Castellini in a statement.

For generations, baseball, and Major League Baseball (MLB) have captivated the hearts of millions as America's favorite pastime. With a rich history of unforgettable moments and a legacy of legendary figures, the sport has become a mainstay in the fabric of American culture.

However, that is not to say that in recent years, MLB has faced mounting challenges in maintaining its relevance in an increasingly fast-paced and competitive world. As younger generations find themselves drawn to other forms of entertainment and the sport grapples with its own captive issues, there is still no doubt that the sport and future of baseball need the attention that comes from the comprehensive general management of every team.

Hopefully, this book has given you what you need every Monday morning while on the couch in your favorite baseball cave to watch and enjoy the game with a new perspective. We just touched on many topics. A whole separate book could be written about many and most of these chapter topics.

Sports Entrepreneur at sportsentrepreneur.com, a digital sports media brand and production company for entrepreneurs engaged in sports, summed it up best by reporting, "The future of Major League Baseball depends on its leaders' willingness to listen, innovate, adapt, and preserve the essence of the sport while embracing the realities of our modern world. By tackling these challenges head-on, they can ensure that America's pastime continues to captivate and inspire generations to come, maintaining its rightful place in our hearts and in our culture. The time is now to embrace change and carry the legacy of baseball into a new era, where the crack of the bat and the roar of the crowd remain the soundtrack of countless summers to come."

About the Author

Al Lautenslager, a resident of Phoenix, Arizona, is an eight-times published, best-selling author, entrepreneur, book collector, businessperson, and professional speaker, passionate about baseball.

Currently, Al is enjoying a retired life pursuing his passions of baseball, travel, writing, and family life. He is also a SABR member.

His baseball passion has extended to his working as a Spring Training Usher for the Cincinnati Reds and Cleveland Guardians at Goodyear Ballpark in Goodyear, Arizona.

Al's visits to any ballpark, major or minor league, on his travels make him the ultimate baseball fan.

Al has the ability to tell stories necessary to connect with his audiences. From his personal experiences, he turns facts and chronology into innovative narratives. It is this quality that can also be seen in the writing of Managing the Show.

He is a well-known business author and contributor. Since his youth, he has been an avid baseball fan, either as a spectator or a player.

Growing up in Cincinnati before, during, and after the days of the Big Red Machine, Al put together a string of 10 straight Cincinnati Red opening day game attendances. Opening Day in Cincinnati is a holiday. Al treated it as such and still marks the day on his calendar. Interviewing the General Manager of the Reds was one of the highlights of the writing of this book.

He has visited over half of the Major League Baseball ballparks during his travels, in addition to visits to over a dozen minor league games and parks.

In 1983, Al drove to Philadelphia, attended game 4 of the World Series against the Baltimore Orioles, and returned to his home in Dayton, Ohio, all in 24 hours' time just because he was passionate about seeing the World Series Game that year. He has been to All-Star games and attended the very first game in the new Comiskey Park in Chicago. The General Managers in baseball have produced these products.

In 1993, on a return plane trip from St. Louis to Chicago, Al had the privilege of sitting next to and enjoying a one-on-one conversation with Hall of Famer Lou Brock. Lou and Al talked about Pete Rose, the trade that Lou Brock took from Chicago to St. Louis, the hall of fame ring on his finger, and even life outside of baseball. This plane ride was a dream come true for any baseball fan, and Al could live that dream. Lou did not share any General Manager stories.

Al met Pete Rose on the day he hit his Ty Cobb, 4192 record-breaking hit and was at the game where Pete hit number 4256, his last Major League hit. In his home library, under a framed picture of the old Crosley Field in Cincinnati, his current baseball book collection contains every Pete Rose book ever written, as well as many volumes by Roger Angell, Roger Kahn, Bill James, Jonathan Eig, George Will, and many, many other baseball writers.

Al is an accomplished businessman, speaker, and communicator and understands the value of good publicity and promotion. As a result, he has built close ties to the media, sports contacts, authorities, and opinion makers.

For more details, contact al@allautenslager.com.

Made in the USA
Monee, IL
05 May 2025

16884372R00162